THE
Life
OF
WASHINGTON

CROSSING THE DELAWARE

In order to preserve the historical nature of this work, British spellings and the formatting of the text have been kept as they were in the original book as found.

First printing: November 2009

Copyright © 2009 by Attic Books. All rights reserved. No part of this book may be used or reproduced in any manner whatsoever without written permission of the publisher, except in the case of brief quotations in articles and reviews.

For information write:
New Leaf Publishing Group, P.O. Box 726, Green Forest, AR 72638.

ISBN-13: 978-0-89051-578-5
ISBN-10: 0-89051-578-6
Library of Congress Number: 2009910387

Printed in the United States of America

Please visit our website for other great titles: www.nlpg.com

Originally published in 1842 by:

American Sunday-School Union

Now known as:

American Missionary Fellowship

http://www.americanmissionary.org/

TABLE OF CONTENTS

ADVERTISEMENT.

The historical portion of this volume is extracted from the best authorities; but it has been deemed unnecessary to introduce references.

PUBLISHER'S NOTE

Anna C. Reed, niece of a signer of the Declaration of Independence, authored this amazing work for the ASSU prior to 1850. Originally translated into over 20 languages within a few years, the book was among the most widely-read biographies of Washington at the time.

The ASSU, now called American Missionary Fellowship (AMF), has been associated with some of America's most prominent citizens and religious leaders. Bushrod Washington, George Washington's nephew and heir of Mount Vernon, who served as Associate Justice of the US Supreme Court, was vice-president of the ASSU until his death in 1829. Included among other ASSU officers or influenced by its mission were Bishop William White of Philadelphia's Christ Church; Francis Scott Key, who wrote "The Star Spangled Banner"; D.L. Moody; Laura Ingalls Wilder; and John Adams (related to both early American presidents), who personally organized over 320 Sunday schools.

ASSU missionaries carried books published by the mission in saddlebags to leave with the fledgling Sunday schools they had started, promoting literacy, education, and the very best in Christian moral values. Though it stopped publishing books in 1968, American Missionary Fellowship continues its missionary work in the United States, extending beyond Sunday school work to include church planting, church camps, and numerous other programs.

http://www.americanmissionary.org/

INTRODUCTION.

In the year 1486, a foot traveller, holding a boy by the hand, stopped at the gate of a convent in Spain, to ask for some bread and water for his wearied child. While he was receiving it from a kind Friar, he gave him a history of himself, and told him for what purpose he had come into that country. At that time, the inhabitants of Europe, Asia, and Africa, did not know that there was any other land than those continents, and some islands not very distant from them.

The most learned men, who were endeavouring to increase their knowledge of geography, thought that the ocean surrounded those countries like a great belt, and *Christopher Columbus*, the stranger who stood at the convent gate, was perhaps the first person who thought that belt might be crossed to the land on the opposite side ; which was supposed to be the eastern part of Asia. He was born about the year 1436, and was the son of a wool-comber, who lived in a city of Italy, called Genoa, and who was too poor to give him much education ; but Columbus was very attentive to the instructions which he received in the few years that he went to school. When he was a child, he said he would like to be a sailor, and he was very diligent in

using every opportunity to gain a knowledge
of geography and navigation.

At the age of fourteen, he went to sea. A
seafaring life was, at that time, a very dangerous and toilsome one ; and the years of his
boyhood were passed in hardships, which
were severe but useful lessons to teach him to
command his naturally hasty temper, and to
endure sufferings without shrinking or com-
plaining. He reflected on what he observed
in his voyages, and on what he had learned
of geography, and felt convinced, that if a
vessel sailed from Europe towards the west,
it might reach a land which was then unknown ; and that land he thought it was probable was an inhabited one. The Bible would
have taught him that a time will come when
' All the ends of the earth shall see the salva-
tion of our God," and he might then have felt
the religious hope that he should be permitted
to carry the glad tidings to the unknown land,
the discovery of which he began to speak of
with as much certainty as if he had seen it.
He considered his almost infant desire to become a sailor as a proof that he was thus early
preparing to be the discoverer of that land ; and
this confidence never left his mind, but cheered
him in his darkest hours of disappointment.

He thought deeply on the subject for many
years, and at length resolved to undertake a
voyage of discovery, which the more he
thought of, the stronger became his hope that it

would be successful. He was too poor to fit out even a small vessel, and he could not persuade any person to assist him in what was considered a wild and useless project. He formed the bold resolution to go to Portugal, and ask assistance from the king, who at first seemed willing to grant it; but after raising his hopes, disappointed them, and Columbus returned to his own country, and made an application there to the government for aid; but his request was disregarded. Poor as to earthly treasures, but trusting to the divine promise, " Commit thy works unto the Lord, and thy thoughts shall be established," he persevered in his intention, and was on his way to seek assistance from Ferdinand and Isabella, the king and queen of Spain, when he stopped at the convent gate to ask for refreshment for his child, whom he was taking with him.

The kind man, to whom he related his plan, became interested for his success, and offered to keep his son, Diego, and educate him; and said he would give him a letter to a friend, who he thought could assist him to gain the favour of the queen. Columbus left his son with him, and travelled to the city where the king and queen resided. They would not even listen to his proposal to discover a new country for them, but he determined to remain there for some time, and he supported himself by designing maps. He was very pleasing in his appearance, and being master of his hasty temper, his manners were agreeable. In a short time, he gained the good will of some persons who interested themselves for him, and introduced him to the Archbishop of Spain, to relate to him the favourite subject of his thoughts. The Archbishop obtained permission for him to appear before the king and queen, and the favourable manner in which they listened to him, gave him lively hopes that they would grant to him the assistance which he desired. They appointed persons to examine his plan for a voyage of discovery, who kept him for a long time uncertain as to what opinion they would give, and then said that they disapproved of it entirely.

Discouraged, but not despairing, Columbus resolved to leave Spain, and seek assistance elsewhere, and was on his journey when he received a letter from a friend, desiring him to return immediately. That friend had succeeded in gaining permission to speak to the queen, and he had interested her so much by an eloquent account of the views of Columbus, that she said, "I undertake the enterprise, and pledge my jewels to raise the necessary funds." These were joyful words to the ear of Columbus; and they were not vain words; for an order, signed by the king and queen, was given to him to enable him to fit out three caravals, or small vessels, for his voyage. They were to be prepared at the

town of Palos, and such frightful tales were
there told about the dangers of the unknown
deep, that even old seamen spoke of the intended voyage with dread; and Columbus
had great difficulty to obtain crews for his
little vessels.

On Friday, the third day of August, in the
year 1492, he sailed from Palos, and the
friends of the sailors who accompanied him
took leave of them with lamentations, and
abuse of Columbus; for they felt certain his
little fleet would never return. It was borne
across the waves for several weeks, and no
tokens of land appeared. The sailors became
very anxious and discontented. One evening, a long dusky strip, like land, excited
glad expectations, but the dawn of the next
day showed that it was only a gray cloud
along the horizon. They were several times
disappointed in the same manner, and at
length became desponding, and reproached
Columbus with anger, and insisted that he
should turn back towards Spain. He tried
to soothe them, and encourage them to go on;
but finding that their desire to give up the
voyage increased, he told them resolutely,
"Happen what will, I am determined to
persevere, until, by the blessing of God, I
shall accomplish the enterprise." When he
had made this declaration, his sailors became
desperate, and resolved to force him to com-
ply with their wishes. While they were

planning how they should do so, on the 11th
October, being sixty-nine days since their
sailing, some fresh grass, such as grows in
rivers, floated by the ships, and one of the
sailors drew up a carved staff, and a thorn
branch with berries on it, which the waves
dashed against the side of the vessel.

As the olive leaf, which God sent to Noah
by the dove, cheered him in his ark with the
hope that he should soon behold " the dry
land," so, the carved staff and thorn-stem
gave Columbus the expectation that he was
drawing near to the land which was the object of his perilous voyage. To the sailors
they were peace branches ; for the hopes they
raised that an inhabited country was not far
distant, quieted their angry feelings, and each
one became engaged in watching for land,
that he might give the first signal of discovery ;
for which a reward had been promised. The
little fleet was moved rapidly on by a fresh
breeze, which blew all day.

It was the custom of Columbus to close
each day with an evening hymn, for he was
a devout man ; and on the evening of that joy-
ous day, on which the staff and thorn stem
were seen, he spoke with great feeling to his
sailors, and endeavoured to lead them to be
grateful to the mighty Ruler of the waves,
for his protection and goodness in guiding
them safely to that hour of cheering hope.
He then seated himself at the end of his ves·

sel, and as it was borne along swiftly by the breeze, his eyes were fixed in watchfulness on the dusky horizon, until it was hid by the darkness of night. His anxiety prevented all disposition to sleep, and as he sat, with the silence of midnight around him, suddenly a light appeared, which seemed like a torch in the hand of a person, raising and lowering it as he walked. Long, very long, no doubt, appeared the hours from that moment until the dawning of the day. At length that dawn came. It was the 12th of October, in the year 1492, and the little vessel of Columbus became to him what " the mountain of Nebo," was to the leader of Israel; for as Moses had been led through the dangers of the wilderness, to that mount from which he saw " the promised land," so Columbus had been guided by the same mighty hand over the desert of the ocean, to a spot from which his joyful eyes beheld the unknown land, on which his thoughts and hopes had been for many years engaged. It was a beautiful level island, covered with trees like an orchard, and the inhabitants were soon seen running towards the shore, to gaze at the wonderful sight which was presented by the little fleet of Columbus. He entered his small boat, and was rowed to the rural spot ; he sprung on it with joy, and kneeled down to offer thanksgiving to God with tears of gratitude. As he approached, the wild natives fled ; but one of

them, more courageous than the rest, ventured
to return ; and others, seeing that he was not
harmed, soon joined him.   They expressed
their astonishment by making signs that they
thought Columbus and his companions had
come from the sky, and that the sails of the
vessels were the wings on which they had
flown down. He remained all the day amidst
the refreshing groves, noticing the artless natives, and giving to them glass beads, and other
trifles, which they received with wonder and
gladness, and brought in return cakes, formed
from the roots of a plant which they cultivated in their fields.   They had ornaments
of gold around their necks, and made Columbus understand that they got them from a
country to the south of their island.   As he
thought that the island was near India, he
called the natives Indians ; and that name has
been continued to all the original inhabitants
of the new world.   He gave the name of
San Salvador to the island ; it is one of the
cluster which is now called the Bahamas.

When he had spent two days in examining
the island, he determined to sail again and
visit others, which he understood from the
natives, were not distant.   He continued sailing in different directions, and discovered the
islands of Cuba and Hispaniola ; he then returned to Spain, and entered the port of Palos,
March 15, 1493, after an absence of 7 months
and 12 days. When the inhabitants heard of

his arrival, there was a great tumult; and
when they knew he had discovered " the unknown land," and that some of the natives
had willingly returned with him, they were
ready to receive him with such honours as
they would have paid to the king. What a
contrast to the time of his departure, when
every tongue was uttering lamentations or
abuse !

When the king and queen heard of his return and success, they ordered great preparations to be made for welcoming him, and he
was every where surrounded by a wondering
and admiring multitude. Who would have
thought that he was the same Columbus, who
but a few years before, had stood at the convent gate, begging bread and water for his
child ! In the course of the next twelve years
he made four very important voyages, and in
honour of him, all the newly found world
should have been called Columbia. He was
deprived of this distinction, by a rich merchant of Italy, Amerigo Vespucio, who sailed
with a large fleet, in 1501, and aided by the
publications and maps of Columbus, reached
a more southern part of the continent than the
great discoverer, and gave so interesting an
account of his voyage, and of the country he
had seen, that his name was given to it, as if
the discovery were his. But the people have
given the names Columbia and Columbus to

several places in America, especially in the
United States, where there is a district called
Columbia, in which is the city of Washington,
the seat of government.   Thus the names of
the two great men are connected, to whose
genius and virtue our country owes so much.

While he was engaged in making discoveries, Columbus endured various trials of mind,
and toils of body ; and after all his faithful services, the king of Spain refused even to furnish him the means of paying his seamen, for
whom he pleaded earnestly, although many
of them had acted as his enemies.   The
amiable queen, Isabella, was an unchanged
friend ; but she died, and then it was vain for
Columbus to ask for justice.   He wrote to a
friend, that he had done all in his power, and
that he left the result to God, who had never
forsaken him in his time of need. In his
seventieth year, he felt that all his cares
would soon cease, and he settled his earthly
affairs and prepared for death.   He charged
his children to be active in spreading abroad
the Christian religion ; and on the 20th of May
1506, he uttered his last words, which were,
" Into thy hands, O Lord, I commend my
spirit."

The accounts which had been published
by Columbus, caused many nations to desire
to have possession of some portions of the
new world.   French, Dutch, and English

navigators made voyages of discovery, and
claimed those parts on which they landed ;
and their governments made settlements on
them. In the year 1496, John Cabot had the
command of a small English fleet, with which
he sailed to the west, and discovered a large
island, which his sailors called Newfound-
land. He then sailed along the coast of North
America, for some distance, but did not land.
Several attempts were afterwards made by the
English to form settlements in it, but they
were not successful until April, 1607, when
one hundred and five of them landed in Virginia, and built a town, which they called
Jamestown, in honour of their king.

One of the most active of those settlers
was Captain Smith, who gained the good will
of all the natives near the settlement ; but being
one day at some distance from it, he was
seized by a party of strange Indians, and taken
to their king, Powhatan. It was determined
that the prisoner should be put to death by
having his head beat with clubs. He was
laid on a large stone, and the death clubs were
raised, when Pocahontas, the daughter of the
king, threw herself beside him, and folding
her arms around him, laid her head on his, and
entreated that his life might be spared. She
was only thirteen years of age, and was the
darling of her father, who consented to her
request, and Captain Smith was permitted to

return to Jamestown. Some time after, she was married, with the consent of her father, to a young Englishman, named Rolfe, and this secured Powhatan as a faithful and powerful friend to the settlers. Pocahontas professed belief in the Christian religion, and was baptized by the name of Rebecca.

In 1620, the second English settlement in North America was made. A number of families, who were not at liberty to worship God as they thought right, went over to Holland. They were kindly received, and had remained there for ten years, supporting themselves by their industry, when they resolved, after frequent and serious prayer, to cross the Atlantic, and seek a residence in America; the evil examples and corrupt manners that prevailed being such as they feared might lead their offspring astray. One hundred and one arrived, like pilgrims, in the beginning of winter, (Nov. 11, 1620,) in a strange country, where there was no friend to welcome them, nor shelter for them to enter. They purchased land from the Indians in Massachusetts, and began to clear a spot for a town, which they called New Plymouth. They endured, with resolute cheerfulness, the toils and dangers of forming homes in a wilderness, because they believed that God would "not leave them, nor forsake them." They desired to "worship him in spirit and in truth," and trusted in his pro-

mise that " all things should work together
for their good.

Other settlements were gradually made in
different parts of the country. Maryland was
colonized in 1633, under Lord Baltimore.
The settlers of Connecticut received a charter
in 1662, from King Charles II. permitting the
people to make their own laws, and in 166
similar rights were given to Rhode-Island,
both of which provinces were settled by independent colonies, chiefly from Massachusetts.
The country now forming the states of North
Carolina, South Carolina, and Georgia were
granted to Lord Clarendon and others, in 1663.
New York and New Jersey, which had been
previously occupied by the Dutch, were granted
by King Charles to his brother, the Duke of
York, and were easily subdued by the English. In October, 1682, William Penn, from
whom Pennsylvania was named, brought from
England a number of families, who had been
persecuted on account of their religious opinions. He purchased land for them from the
Indians, who kindly taught them how to
make sodded huts, on the spot where Philadelphia now stands. Each settlement was
called a Province, and the inhabitants made
regulations for their own government, but
acknowledged themselves to be subjects of
the king of England. Those who had fled
from their native land, that they might wor-

ship God with freedom, believed that they should have fulfilled to them His promise which they found in the Scriptures—" Though I have scattered them, yet I will be unto them as a little sanctuary in the countries where they shall come."

LIFE OF WASHINGTON

CHAPTER I.

1732—1762.

To give us the delightful assurance, that we are always under the watchful care of our almighty and kind Creator, He has told us that He notices the movements of every little sparrow ; and as we are " of more value than many sparrows," He will surely ever care for us. It was His powerful and kind care that protected and guided Columbus, the once poor sailor boy, to obtain the favour of a great king and queen ; and then to pass over the waves of a dangerous ocean, in a little vessel, and reach in safety an unknown land. The same powerful and kind care which protected and guided houseless strangers to a land of freedom and peace, gave Washington to their children, to lead them on to take a place amongst the nations of the earth. His history is as a shining light upon the path of virtue ; for he " acknowledged God in all his ways."

George Washington was the third son of Augustine Washington, whose grandfather

left England, his native country, in 1657, and
settled at Bridges Creek, in Virginia, where,
on the 22d of February, in the year 1732, his
great-grandson, George, was born.*

One of the first lessons which young Washington received from his faithful parents, was,
the importance of always speaking the truth;
and they enjoyed a satisfactory reward for
their attention to this duty; for through his
childhood, "the law of truth was in his
mouth," so that he was not known in one instance to tell a falsehood, either to obtain a
desired indulgence, or to escape a deserved
punishment or reproof. His character, as a
lover of truth, was so well known at the school
which he attended, that the children were
certain of being believed, when they related
any thing, if they could say, "George Washington says it was so."

An anecdote is related of him to illustrate
this trait in his character, which we introduce
without being able to ascertain on what authority it is related. We hope it will not be
supposed, however, that we regard such an
incident as an extraordinary proof of ingenu-
ousness on the part of young Washington.
We trust there are very few boys who would
think of adopting any other course under like

* The birth-day of Washington was the eleventh February, 1732, according to the dates used at that time,
but, as in the year 1752, the English dates were altered
to conform with those of the rest of Europe, the day is
that which is here given, twenty-second February, 1732.

circumstances, and those who do generally find that "honesty is the best policy," to say nothing of a quiet conscience and the law of God.

The story is, that he was playing with a hatchet, and heedlessly struck a favourite fruit-tree in his father's garden. Upon seeing the tree thus mutilated, an inquiry was naturally made for the author of the mischief, when George frankly confessed the deed, and received his father's forgiveness.

In all the little disputes of the school-fellows, he was called on to say which party was right, and his decisions were always satisfactory.

It is, perhaps, not out of place to remark in this connexion, that much of the injustice and oppression which are seen in the intercourse of men with each other, shows only the maturity of habits which were formed in childhood. At home, or in school, or on the play-ground, instances of unfairness and fraud are often seen, which, among men, would be regarded as gross violations of law and right. Washington in his boyhood was JUST.

When he was ten years old, his worthy father died, and he became the care of an anxious mother, whose fortune was not sufficient to enable her to give him more than a plain English education. He was very fond of studying mathematics, and applied his mind

diligently, in improving all the instruction
which he could get in that science. As he
grew up to manhood, he was remarkable for
the strength and activity of his frame. In
running, leaping, and managing a horse, he
was unequalled by his companions ; and he
could with ease climb the heights of his native mountains, to look down alone from some
wild crag upon his followers, who were pant-
ing from the toils of the rugged way. By
these healthful exercises the vigour of his
constitution was increased, and he gained that
hardiness so important to him in the employments designed for him by his Creator.

Mrs. Washington was an affectionate parent; but she did not encourage in herself
that imprudent tenderness, which so often
causes a mother to foster the passions of her
children by foolish indulgences, and which
seldom fails to destroy the respect which
every child should feel for a parent. George
was early made to understand that he must
obey his mother, and therefore he respected
as well as loved her. She was kind to his
young companions, but they thought her stern,
because they always felt that they must behave correctly in her presence. The character
of the mother, as well as that of the son, are
shown in the following incident. Mrs. Washington owned a remarkably fine colt, which
she valued very much ; but which, though
old enough for use, had never been mounted;

no one would venture to ride it, or attempt to break its wild and vicious spirit. George proposed to some of his young companions, that they should assist him to secure the colt until he could mount it, as he had determined that he would try to tame it. Soon after sun rise, one morning, they drove the wild animal into an enclosure, and with great difficulty succeeded in placing a bridle on it. George then sprang upon its back, and the vexed colt bounded over the open fields, prancing and plunging to get rid of his burden. The bold rider kept his seat firmly, and the struggle between them became alarming to his companions, who were watching him. The speed of the colt increased, until at length, in making a furious effort to throw his conqueror, he burst a large blood-vessel, and instantly died. George was unhurt, but was much troubled by the unexpected result of his exploit. His companions soon joined him, and when they saw the beautiful colt lifeless, the first words they spoke were, "What will your mother say—who can tell her?" They were called to breakfast, and soon after they were seated at the table, Mrs. Washington said, "Well, young gentlemen, have you seen my fine sorrel colt in your rambles?" No answer was given, and the question was repeated; her son George then replied—"Your sorrel colt is dead, mother." He gave her an exact account of the event. The flush of displeasure which first rose on her cheek, soon passed away; and she said calmly, " While I regret the loss of my favourite, *I rejoice in my son, who always speaks the truth.*"

In his fifteenth year, he had so strong a desire to be actively employed, that he applied for a place as a midshipman in the English navy, (for our country was then under the government of Great Britain,) and succeeded in obtaining it. Full of youthful expectations of enjoyment in a new scene, he prepared ardently to engage in it, when he became convinced that by doing so, he would severely wound the heart of an anxious parent; and with a true spirit of heroism he denied himself, and in obedience to the command, " Honour thy mother," he gave up his fondly cherished plan, and yielded his own inclinations, to promote her comfort. Thus, while his manly superiority to companions of his own age caused admiration, his filial tenderness was an example to them of compliance with the direction which is given to children in the word of God. " Let them learn first to show piety at home, and to requite their parents," and they are assured that " this is good and acceptable to the Lord." Washington proved the truth of this assurance; for, to the act of filial regard which " requited" the anxious cares of his mother, may be traced his usefulness to his country, and the glory of his character. If he had crossed his mother's wish, and entered the British navy as a midshipman, it is not probable, that he would ever have deserved, or obtained, the title of " Father of his country."

Being unwilling to remain inactive, young Washington employed himself industriously and usefully in surveying unsettled lands ; and when he was nineteen years of age, he was appointed one of the adjutant generals of Virginia, with the rank of a major. At that time, the French nation had large settlements in Canada, and in Louisiana, and they determined on connecting those settlements by a line of forts ; in doing this they took possession of a tract of land, which was considered to be within the province of Virginia. The governor of Virginia, (Mr. Dinwiddie) thought it was his duty to notice this, in the name of his king; and it was very important, that the person whom he employed in the business. should have resolution and prudence. Young Washington was worthy of his confidence, and willingly undertook the perilous duty ; as it gave him an opportunity of being actively employed for the advantage of his native province. The dangers which he knew he must meet, did not, for a moment, deter him from consenting to set out immediately on the toilsome journey, although winter was near. He was to take a letter from the governor, to the commanding officer of the French troops, who were stationed on the Ohio river; and the way he had to go, was through a part of the country that had never been furrowed by the plough, or, indeed, marked by any footsteps, but those of wild animals, or ferocious Indians. Many of those Indians were enemies, and those who had shown any disposition to be friendly, could not be safely trusted.

The same day, (October 31, 1753,) on which Washington received the letter which he was to be the bearer of, he left Williamsburgh, and travelled with speed until he arrived at the frontier settlement of the province ; and there engaged a guide to show him the way over the wild and rugged Alleghany mountain, which, at that season of the year, it was difficult to pass. The waters to be crossed were high, and the snow to be waded through, was deep ; but persevering resolutely, he arrived at Turtle Creek, where he was told by an Indian trader, that the French commander had died a short time before, and that the French troops had gone into winter quarters.

He went on with increased ardour, because the difficulty of his duty was increased ; but he did not neglect the opportunity of examining the country through which he passed ; wishing to discover the best situations on which forts could be erected for the defence of the province.

As the waters were impassable without swimming the horses, he got a canoe to take the baggage about ten miles, to the forks of

Washington Crossing the Alleghanies.

the Ohio river; intending to cross the Alleghany there. In his journal he wrote, " as I got down before the canoe, I spent some time in viewing the rivers and the land in the fork which I think extremely well suited for a fort, as it has the absolute command of both rivers. The land at the point is twenty or twentyfive feet above the common surface."

The spot thus described was soon afterwards the site of the French fort Duquesne. It was subsequently called fort Pitt by the English, and from this the name of the town of Pittsburg was taken, which was built near the fort, and is now a city, containing 22,000 inhabitants. Washington remained a few days in that neighbourhood, for the purpose of endeavouring to persuade the Indian warriors to be friendly to the English. By a firm but mild manner, he gained friends among the inhabitants of the forest, and obtained guides to conduct him by the shortest way to the fort, where he expected to find a French officer, to whom he might give the letter from the governor, as the commander was dead.

He arrived there in safety, and when he had received an answer from the officer, set out immediately on his return, and the journey proved a very dangerous and toilsome one. Some extracts from his journal, which he kept with exactness, will show his disregard of self, when he was performing a duty for the benefit of others. He had put on an In-

dian walking dress, and given his horse to assist in carrying provisions ; the cold increased
very much and the roads were getting worse
every day, from the freezing of a deep snow,
so that the horses became almost unable to
travel. After describing this difficulty, he
wrote thus:—

" As I was uneasy to get back, to make a
report of my proceedings to his honour the
governor, I determined to prosecute my journey the nearest way, through the woods, on
foot. I took my necessary papers, pulled off
my clothes, and tied myself up in a watch
coat. Then, with gun in hand and pack on
my back, in which were my papers and provisions, I set out with Mr. Gist, fitted in the
same manner. We fell in with a party of In
dians, who had laid in wait for us. One of
them fired, not fifteen steps off, but fortunately
missed ; we walked on the remaining part of
the night, without making any stop, that we
might get the start so far, as to be out of the
reach of their pursuit the next day, as we
were well assured that they would follow our
track as soon as it was light. The next day
we continued travelling until quite dark, and
got to the river. We expected to have found
the river frozen, but it was not, only about
fifty yards from each shore. The ice I suppose had been broken up, for it was driving
in vast quantities. There was no way of getting over but on a raft ; which we set about

making, with but one poor hatchet, and finished just after sun-setting: this was a whole
day's work. We got it launched, then went
on board of it, and set off; but before we
were half-way over, we were jammed in the
ice in such a manner, that we expected every
moment our raft to sink, and ourselves to
perish. I put out my setting pole to try to
stop the raft, that the ice might pass by, when
the rapidity of the stream threw it with so
much violence against the pole, that it jerked
me out into ten feet water."

In this dangerous situation he was saved by
the protecting hand of God, and enabled again
to get on the raft; and by the next morning,
the river was frozen so hard, that there was
no difficulty in getting to the shore on the ice.
The remainder of the journey was very fatiguing, being in the month of December, and
for fifteen days it either snowed or rained.

He arrived the 16th of January at Williamsburgh, and delivered the important letter to
the governor. The answer of the French
officer, which was contained in the letter, was
such as to make needful immediate preparations for defending the frontier of the province.
The resolution with which Washington had
performed the duty entrusted to him, and the
judgment he had shown in his conduct towards the Indians, gained the favourable opinion of the people of the province, as well as
that of the governor, and he was appointed a

lieutenant-colonel of the regiment which was formed to march to the frontier, in order to prevent the French erecting their forts on it. Ardent and active, he obtained permission to march with two companies, in advance of the regiment, to a place called the Great Meadows, he thought that in doing so, he would have an opportunity of getting early information as to the movements of the French, and of forming a treaty with the Indians, to prevent their joining them. On arriving there, he was informed, by an Indian, that the French commander had sent a party to stop the American workmen, who were erecting a fort; and that they were forming one for themselves, called fort Duquesne. The Indian also gave the information, that French troops were advancing from that fort towards the Great Meadows. The night on which this account was given, was dark and rainy; but Washington marched rapidly with his soldiers to the place where the Indian said the French would be encamped; and there he found them, and surrounded them so unexpectedly, that they gave themselves up as his prisoners. The chief officer of that part of the regiment which was marching slowly on, died; and Washington then had the entire command of about four hundred men. They joined him, and he directed them to form a shelter for their horses and provisions; when it was completed, they named it fort Necessity.

After placing the horses and baggage in it, Washington marched with his troops towards fort Duquesne, for the purpose of endeavouring to drive the French from it; but when he had advanced about thirteen miles, an Indian told him, that there were " as many Frenchmen coming towards him, as there were pigeons in the woods;" and he thought it was most prudent to return to his little fort, and meet their attack there. He returned, and assisted his men in digging a ditch round the fort, and while they were thus engaged, about fifteen hundred French and Indians made their appearance, and soon began to attack them. The ditch was not sufficiently completed to be of any use. The Indians sent their arrows from behind the surrounding trees, and the French fired from the shelter of the high grass. Washington continued outside of the little fort, directing and aiding his soldiers, from ten o'clock until dark, when the French commander made an offer to cease the attack, if the fort would be given up to him. The conditions he first named, Washington would not agree to ; but at last, the French commander consented to allow the troops to march out with their baggage, and return to the inhabited part of the province, and Washington then gave up the fort. He returned to Williamsburgh, and the courage with which he had acted, and the favourable terms he had obtained from so large a force, increased the confidence

of his countrymen in his character. This occurrence took place on the third of July, 1754.

In the course of the next winter, orders
were received, that officers who had commis-
sions from the king, should be placed above
those belonging to the province, without regard
to their rank. The feeling of what was due to
him as an American, prevented Washington
from submitting to this unjust regulation, and
he resigned his commission. Many letters were
written to him, to persuade him not to do so ;
and he answered them, with an assurance
that he would " serve willingly, when he
could do so without dishonour." His eldest
brother had died, and left to him a farm called
Mount Vernon, situated in Virginia, near the
Potomac river ; he took possession of it, and
began to employ himself industriously in its
cultivation. While he was thus engaged,
General Braddock was sent from England, to
prepare and command troops for the defence
of Virginia, through the summer. Hearing of
the conduct of Washington as an officer, and
of his reasons for giving up his commission,
he invited him to become his aid-de-camp.
He accepted the invitation, on condition that
he might be permitted to return to his farm
when the active duties of the campaign should
be over.

The army was formed of two regiments of
British troops, and a few companies of Virginians. The third day after the march com-

menced, Washington was taken ill, with a
violent fever. He would not consent to be left
behind, and was laid in a covered wagon. He
thought that it was very important to reach
the frontier as soon as possible, and he knew
the difficulties of the way; he therefore proposed to General Braddock, who asked his
advice, to send on a part of the army, while
the other part moved slowly, with the artillery and baggage wagons. Twelve hundred
men were chosen, and General Braddock accompanied them; but though not cumbered
with baggage, their movements did not satisfy
Washington. He wrote to his brother, that,
" instead of pushing on with vigour, without
minding a little rough road, they were halting
to level every molehill, and erect bridges over
every brook." What seemed mountains to
them, were molehills to the ardent temper of
Washington. His illness increased so much,
that the physician said his life would be en-
dangered by going on, and General Braddock
would not suffer him to do so, but gave him
a promise to have him brought after him, so
soon as he could bear the ride. He recovered
sufficiently, in a short time, to join the advanced troops; and though very weak, entered
immediately on the performance of his duties.

General Braddock proceeded on his march
without disturbance, until he arrived at the
Monongahela river, about seven miles from
Fort Duquesne. As he was preparing to

cross the river, at the place since called Braddock's Ford, a few Indians were seen on the
opposite shore, who made insulting gestures,
and then turned and fled as the British troops
advanced.   Braddock gave orders that the Indians should be pursued.   Colonel Washington was well acquainted with the manner in
which the French, assisted by Indians, made
their attacks; and being aware of the danger
into which the troops might be led, he earnestly entreated General Braddock not to proceed, until he should, with his Virginia rangers, search the forest. His proposal offended
Braddock, who disregarded the prudent counsel, and ordered his troops to cross the river;
the last of them were yet wading in it, when
the bullets of an unseen enemy thinned the
ranks of those who had been incautiously led
into the entrance of a hollow, where the French
and Indians were concealed by the thick under-
wood, from which they could securely fire on
the English.   In a few moments, the fearful
war-whoop was sounded, and the French and
Indians rushed from their shelter on the astonished troops of Braddock, and pursued them
to the banks of the Monongahela.

In vain did their commander, and the un-
daunted Washington, endeavour to restore
them to order and prevent their flight.   The
deadly aim of the enemy was so sure, that in
a very short time Washington was the only
aid of General Braddock that was left to carry

his orders and assist in encouraging the affrighted troops. For three hours, he was exposed to the aim of the most perfect marks-
men; two horses fell under him; a third was
wounded; four balls pierced his coat, and
several grazed his sword; every other officer
was either killed or wounded, and he alone
remained unhurt. The Indians directed the
flight of their arrows towards his breast, and
the French made him a mark for their rifles,
but both were harmless, for the shield of his
God protected him, and "covered his head in
the heat of battle." His safety, in the midst
of such attacks, astonished his savage enemies,
and they called him "The Spirit-protected
man, who would be a chief of nations, for he
could not die in battle." Thus did even the
Indians own a divine power in his preservation; and the physician, who was on the battle
ground, in speaking of him afterwards, said,
"I expected every moment to see him fall;—
his duty, his situation, exposed him to every
danger; nothing but the superintending care
of Providence could have saved him from the
fate of all around him."—This battle took place
on the 8th of July, 1755. In a note to a sermon preached a month afterwards, by the Rev.
Mr. Davies, of Virginia, (afterwards president
of Princeton College) we find mention made
by the author of "that heroic youth, Colonel
Washington, whom I cannot but hope Providence has hitherto preserved, in so signal a

manner, for some important service to his country."

General Braddock was mortally wounded, and his few remaining soldiers then fled in every direction. But his brave and faithful aid, with about thirty courageous Virginians, remained on the field, to save their wounded commander from the hatchet and the scalping knife of the Indians. They conveyed him with tenderness and speed towards that part of his army which was slowly advancing with the baggage, and he died in their camp, and was buried in the middle of a road, that his grave might be concealed from the Indians by wagon tracks. A few years since, his remains were removed to a short distance, as the great Cumberland road made by the government of the United States, was to pass directly over the spot where he had been laid. More than seventy-five years have passed, since the terrible scene of Braddock's defeat. The plough has since furrowed the ground which was then moistened with the blood of the slain; but it is saddening to see on it white spots of crumbled bones, and to find amidst the green stalks of grain, buttons of the British soldiers, marked with the number of their regiment, even the brazen ornaments of their caps. "Braddock's road," as the path was called, which his troops cut through the forest, is now almost overgrown with bushes; and few travellers pass near to it, without stopping to look along its windings, and recall the time when it was filled with animated soldiers, who were soon to be silenced by the destructive weapons of war.

In writing an account of this dreadful defeat, Washington said, " See the wondrous works of Providence, and the uncertainty of human things !" He was much distressed by the loss of the army : and the officer next in command to General Braddock, instead of endeavouring to prepare for a better defence, went into winter quarters, although it was only the month of August. It was thought necessary to raise more troops immediately, and the command of all that should be raised in Virginia was offered to Washington, with the privilege of naming his own officers. He willingly accepted this offer, as he could do so without placing himself under British commanders, who were not really above him in rank. He immediately set off to visit the troops that had been placed in different situations along the borders of the province : and on his return to prepare for an active defence, he was overtaken by a messenger, with an account, that a number of French troops and Indian warriors, divided into parties, were capturing and murdering the inhabitants of the back settlements,—burning the houses and destroying the crops ; and that the troops stationed there, were unable to protect them.

Washington immediately used every means within his power to provide for their relief; but it was impossible to defend, with a few troops, a frontier of almost four hundred miles, from an enemy that " skulked by day, and plundered by night." While he was anxiously doing what he could, he wrote to the governor an account of the distress around him; and added, " I see their situation,—I know their danger, and participate their sufferings, without having the power to give them further relief than uncertain promises. * * The supplicating tears of the women, and the moving petitions of the men, melt me with deadly sorrow."—It might have been expected, that the people in their distress would blame him for not protecting them better; but no murmur arose against him; they all acknowledged, that he was doing as much for them as was within his power.

He wrote to the lieutenant-governor the most earnest and—pressing requests for more assistance; but instead of receiving it, he was treated unkindly, as he related in a letter to a friend.—" Whence it arises, or why, I am truly ignorant, but my strongest representations of matters, relative to the peace of the frontiers, are disregarded as idle and frivolous; my propositions and measures as partial and selfish; and all my sincerest endeavours for the service of my country, perverted to the worst purposes. My orders are dark, doubtful, and uncertain.—To-day approved, to-morrow condemned ; left to act and proceed at hazard, and blamed without the benefit of defence. However, I am determined to bear up some time longer, in the hope of better regulations."—Though disappointed in all his best formed plans, by the obstinacy and ill-nature of the person who had the power to control him, and pained by the increasing sufferings around him, which he was not enabled to relieve, yet he did not suffer an angry resentment to induce him to give up the effort of doing some good.

He continued his active and humane endeavours, and pleaded for the relief of his suffering countrymen, until his pleadings were called impertinent. In answer to this, he wrote to the governor, " I must beg leave, in justification of my own conduct, to observe, that it is with pleasure I receive reproof, when reproof is due ; because no person can be readier to accuse me than I am to acknowledge an error, when I have committed it ; or more desirous of atoning for a crime, when I am sensible of being guilty of one. But on the other hand, it is with concern I remark, that my conduct, although I have uniformly studied to make it as unexceptionable as I could, does not appear to you in a favourable light."— With calm dignity he endured a continuance of such vexations, without ceasing to toil in his almost hopeless work of humanity.

A new commander of the British troops was sent from England, and he listened to Washington's opinion, that the frontiers could not be freed from the dreadful visits of the Indians, in connection with the French, until they were driven from Fort Duquesne; for that was the place from which they started on their destructive expeditions. When it was determined that this should be attempted, Washington advanced with a few troops, to open the way for the army; but before they reached the fort, the French left it, and the English took possession of it, November 1758, and named it Fort Pitt. As Washington had expected, the possession of this fort prevented all further attacks on the frontiers; and when his countrymen were freed from the dangers which he had left his farm to assist in defending them against, he determined on returning to it. His health had been injured by his being exposed to severe cold, and being often, for many days, unsheltered from the falling rain; and he felt that he ought to use means to restore it, as he could do so without neglecting a more important duty. He resigned his commission, and the officers whom he had commanded united in offering to him affectionate assurances of regret for the loss of " such an excellent commander, such a sincere friend, and so affable a companion."

Soon after his return to his farm, in the

twenty-seventh year of his age, he married Mrs. Custis, a lady to whom he had been long attached, and who was deserving of his affection. She had an amiable temper, and was an agreeable companion; and in performing all the duties of a wife, she made his home a scene of domestic comfort, which he felt no desire to leave. Employing himself in directing the cultivation of his ground, and in the performance of all the private duties of his situation, he lived for several years in retirement, except when attending the legislature of Virginia, of which he was a member.

For the benefit of his health, he sometimes visited a public spring in his native state, to which sick persons went, with the hope of being relieved by using the water. At the season when there were many persons there, it was the custom of a baker to furnish a particular kind of bread, for those who could afford to pay a good price for it. One day it was observed by a visiter, that several miserably poor sick persons tottered into the room where the bread was kept, and looked at the baker, who nodded his head, and each one took up a loaf, and, with a cheerful countenance walked feebly away. The visiter praised the baker for his charitable conduct, in letting those have his bread, whom he knew could never pay him; but he honestly answered, "I lose nothing,—Colonel Washington is here

and all the sick poor may have as much of my
bread as they can eat; he pays the bill, and I
assure you it is no small one."

All his private actions were as deserving
of the approbation of his countrymen, as those
of a public nature had been of their respect
and praise; and those who were nearest to
him, and knew him best, loved him most.

CHAPTER II.

1763—1776.

The desire to possess power, and the ill
use of it when possessed, have caused much
misery in nations, societies, and families; and
even children show the evil effects in over-
bearing conduct to each other, and in delight-
ing to crush the feeble worm which crawls at
their feet. But if that love which fulfils the law
of God were in every heart, the precept of
our divine Redeemer, " All things whatsoever
ye would that men should do to you, do ye
even so to them," would be the rule of all
actions; then families, societies, and nations,
would be ever peaceful. The English government, however, disregarded this precept, and
made an unjust use of their power over the
American provinces. The people paid various

duties on their trade, and made no objection to doing so; but at the close of the war with the French, the English parliament determined on taxing them, for the purpose, they said, of assisting to pay the expenses of the war. The Americans had lost a great number of their young men in that war, and had also contributed their full proportion of money for carrying it on; this new tax, therefore, caused universal displeasure, and they began to think, and to say, that parliament had no right to tax them, as they were not allowed to send members to that body to represent them.

Petitions against the tax were sent to the king and to parliament, but they were disregarded; and in March 1765, a law called the "stamp act," was passed, which was to oblige the Americans in their business transactions, to use paper on which the seal of the British government was stamped. That paper was to be taxed, and no writings of agreement were to be considered binding, unless they were written on stamped paper. The Americans resolutely determined on opposing this tax. In New York the act was printed, and carried about the streets, by the title of "The Folly of England, and the ruin of America;" and when the ships that brought the stamps arrived at Philadelphia, all the vessels in the harbour hoisted their colours half-mast high, as a sign of mourning, and the state-house bell was muffled, and continued to toll until evening.

The same dissatisfaction was felt in all the provinces; and when this was known in England, there were many speeches made on the subject, by members of parliament. One of them, Mr. Grenville, said, the Americans ought not to object to assist in paying the debts of the English government, for they were " children of their planting, and were nourished by their indulgence, and protected by their arms, until they had grown up to a good degree of strength and opulence." Colonel Barré, a member who was desirous that they should be treated justly, said, in answer— " 'Children planted by your care'! No—your oppression planted them in America! They fled from your tyranny into a then uncultivated land, where they were exposed to all the hardships to which human nature is liable. 'They nourished by your indulgence!' No—they grew by your neglect! When you began to care about them, that care was exercised in sending persons to rule over them, whose behaviour, on many occasions, has caused the blood of those sons of liberty to boil within them! 'They protected by your arms!' They have nobly taken up arms in your defence; have exerted their valour amidst their constant and laborious industry, for the defence of a country, the interior of which, while its frontiers were drenched in blood. has yielded all its little savings to your enlargement." His appeal, however, had no effect, and the eloquence of the great Earl of Chatham, with the efforts of other patriots in England, availed as little in stopping the mad career of the British government in its oppressive acts.

The assembly of Massachusetts, proposed a Congress to be held at New York, to consult together on the subject of the right of the English government to tax them. Representatives from nine of the provinces met accordingly, in October 1765, and decided that the colonies alone had the right to lay taxes. This decision was expressed in a petition to the king, and to the parliament. When the parliament found that the resolution to oppose the stamp act, was so general and firm in all the provinces, it was repealed; but as they were determined to show the Americans that they would not give up the power of taxing them, the next year they laid a duty on glass, paints, and tea. Objections and petitions were again sent to parliament, by the Americans, and at length, in 1769, those duties were all taken off, excepting that on tea. While one tax was continued, the Americans would not be satisfied. They were not unwilling to pay it, because they did not wish to part with their money, but because they would not give up the principle that the English government had no just right to it, unless they were allowed to have a part in the government, by sending members to the parliament.

Dr. Franklin, who was highly respected in Europe, not only for his good character, but for his wisdom in making many useful discoveries, was in England, transacting business for some of the inhabitants of Massachusetts, his native province, and he was appointed to present a petition from the assembly of that province to the English government, and was very active in endeavouring to obtain justice for his countrymen. The ill treatment which he there received, much excited the feelings of his countrymen, who held him in the highest regard. As the tax on tea was continued, the Americans resolved not to use any ; and the parliament then made an agreement with the India Tea Company, by which they were to send vessels with tea to the provinces, and receive the duties on it, and then pay it to the English government. But the Americans had resolved to resist the tax, no matter in what way it was laid ; and when the vessels arrived, they would not allow the tea to be landed. The people of Boston were so much displeased, when a vessel with a cargo of tea arrived there, in 1774, that seventeen of the most resolute men went on board, disguised as Indians, and threw all the tea into the sea.

This conduct led the British government to determine on using all their power to punish the Americans, but particularly the inhabitants of Massachusetts ; and they made a law, that the governor and magistrates. and other of-

ficers of that province, should no longer receive their salaries from the people, so as to
be dependent on them—but that they should
be appointed by the king, and paid by him
and that if any persons were accused of mur-
der, or other great crimes, they should not be
tried in the province, but be sent to England
to be tried. When these new laws were
known by the people of the other provinces,
they sent assurances to the people of Massachusetts, that they would unite in assisting
them to resist such injustice. The first of
June, the day on which those laws were to
commence, was appointed by the legislatures
of the different provinces, as one of fasting,
humiliation, and prayer, in which the people
should attend their places of worship, and
unite in asking the support and direction of
God, in that time of public difficulty.

One of the titles given to God is, " Thou
that hearest prayer;" and our divine Redeemer has said, " If ye abide in me, and my
words abide in you, ye shall ask what ye
will, and it shall be done unto you ;" and in
that beautiful parable of the Pharisee and the
Publican, he has set before us an example of
the kind of prayer that would be acceptable to
God. No doubt many pious American hearts
offered such a prayer, with humility and faith
and their prayers were granted ; for they
never would have succeeded in defending
their rights, unless the mighty hand of God

had upheld and guided them. And those who bore the trials of that long and painful contest, proved that love to God, and reliance on his goodness and power, were the best principles of freedom, and led to the noblest sacrifices for their country. They began with prayer, and ended in victory and thanksgiving.

Without any power to call such an assembly, the place and time of meeting were agreed upon with surprising unanimity, and on the 5th of September, 1774, a Congress, composed of delegates from twelve colonies, containing about three million of inhabitants, met at Philadelphia. Washington was one of the members, having been sent by the province of Virginia.

An incident illustrative of Washington's religious habits at this period of his life, is preserved on unquestionable authority. During the session of Congress, a gentleman, residing in the city of Philadelphia, anxious to learn the chief of the strangers who had assembled from the several colonies, observed to Mr. Secretary Thomson, that he had heard much of Mr. Washington from Virginia, and would be glad to know how he could distinguish him. Mr. Thomson replied, " You can easily distinguish him when Congress goes to prayers— *Mr. Washington is the gentleman who kneels down.*" Thus, in the prime of life, did this gentleman, who was as noted for his modesty as for his merit, manifest to the world his sense of the overruling providence of God, and of the power of prayer with him who giveth to all men liberally and upbraideth not.

This incident is particularly worthy of record, as it is evidently undesigned testimony. It is to be lamented that the religious feelings which Washington so uniformly, and yet so unostentatiously exhibited, are not always seen in those who occupy stations of great dignity and importance. There are men who seem to think that a little brief authority on earth sets them above any dependence upon the King of kings and the Lord of lords. WASHINGTON acknowledged God in all his ways.

He had, on all proper occasions, expressed the opinion that the English parliament had no just right to tax the Americans; and he had spoken so firmly on the subject, that he was called "the Virginia Patriot." The Congress appointed committees, to state what the Americans considered to be their rights, and to prepare an address to the people of England, and one to the king. After stating to the king their causes for complaint, they assured him, that they were willing to continue under his government, if their just requests were granted. They said, "We ask but for peace, liberty, and safety; we do not solicit the grant of any new right in our favour." The manner in which this petition was treated, convinced the Americans that they must submit, or prepare for mournful events. The king declared his firm resolve to rule them as he thought best; and General Grant said in Parliament, that he " would undertake to traverse the whole country with five regiments, and drive the inhabitants from one end of the continent to the other."

In all their determinations, the Americans had no intention of commencing a war, but they resolved that if the English attempted to force them into submission, they would resist them. A number of troops were sent from England to Boston, and their commander placed them on Boston Neck, and fortified it for their security. He also seized the American military stores, at several places in the province, and had them conveyed to Boston. When winter approached, he could not get assistance to build a shelter for his troops, and no price that he offered would induce workmen to labour for them ; this convinced him that all the people were of one mind. The winter passed away without any change favourable to the Americans. A considerable quantity of military stores had been collected in the town of Concord, about eighteen miles from Boston. General Gage resolved to destroy them. On the night of the 18th of April, he sent Major Pitcairn, with a detachment of nine hundred men, for this purpose. They marched quietly, and several officers went before, to prevent any one on the road giving notice of their approach. Dr. Warren, however, managed to send a messenger from Boston, to give information at Lexington, where the English troops arrived at five o'clock in the morning of April 19th, and found a company of militia, consisting of seventy men, who were parading under arms. Major Pitcairn rode up to them, and said, " Disperse, rebels; throw down your arms and disperse." The soldiers at the same time ran up, huzzaing; some few guns were fired, which was followed by a general discharge. The firing was continued as long as any of the militia appeared: eight men were killed, and several wounded. The Americans had heretofore suffered and complained, but this was their first active attempt to escape from the unjust exercise of the power which the English possessed. The detachment proceeded to Concord; the commanding officer sent six companies of light infantry to take possession of the bridges which were beyond the town, while the main body were employed in destroying the stores in Concord. Some militia men, who were collected from that place, having orders not to give the first fire, approached one of the bridges as if to pass as common travellers. They were fired on, and two men killed. The fire was returned, and the English were obliged to retreat with loss. The inhabitants of the surrounding country became alarmed by the fearful sounds. The wagoner left his team in the road; the farmer his plough in the furrow; the blacksmith threw down his hammer,—and the young and the old, the strong and the feeble, all rushed towards the sad scene. The king's troops were attacked in every direction, and were driven back to Lexington, where they met a large detachment, with cannon, which had been sent to assist them in case they were resisted. They remained a short time in Lexington, and then recommenced their march. They were closely followed by the Americans, who assailed the invaders, until they arrived, at sun-set, on the common of Charlestown, and then passed over to Bunker's hill, where they were safe for the night, under the protection of their ships of war. The next morning they crossed over Charlestown ferry to Boston.

The English forts at Ticonderoga and Crown Point, having the command of Lake George and Lake Champlain, it was thought very important to the Americans to get possession of them. A number of volunteers from Vermont and Connecticut, commanded by Colonel Ethan Allen and Colonel Benedict Arnold, marched against Ticonderoga, and surprised the garrison, which surrendered without firing a single gun. Colonel Seth Warren was sent to take possession of Crown Point, which he did without meeting with any resistance. When intelligence of these events was brought to Congress, they recommended removing the cannon and military stores to a place of greater safety, and directed that an account should be taken of them, " in order that they might be safely returned, when the restoration of the former harmony between Great Britain and the Colonies, so ardently wished for by the latter, should render it prudent and consistent with the over-ruling law of self-preservation."

After considering all the circumstances of the scene at Lexington, Congress concluded that an American army must be formed for the defence of their country, and this resolve was made public by an address to the people of all the provinces. After relating the causes for their opposition to the English government, and the means that had been used, without effect, to obtain justice, they said, " By one statute it is declared, that Parliament can of right make laws to bind us in all cases whatsoever; not a single man of those who assume this power is chosen by us, or subject to our influence. * * We gratefully acknowledge, as a signal instance of the divine favour towards us, that his providence would not permit us to be called into this severe controversy, until we were grown up to our present strength. We fight not for glory or for conquest. In our native land, in defence of the freedom that is our birth-right, for the protection of our property, acquired solely by the honest industry of our forefathers and our selves, against violence actually offered, we have taken up arms."

Three more English generals arrived at Boston, with troops, and offered pardon to all those who would lay down their arms and submit to the king, with the exception of Samuel Adams and John Hancock, two men who were most distinguished by their ability and zeal in the common cause of their country. This offer made the Americans more active, as it convinced them that there was no hope of safety but in preparation for defence.

As it was expected that General Gage would send troops into the surrounding country, the Americans resolved on raising entrenchments on a height near Boston, called Bunker's hill. A detachment of a thousand men, under the command of Colonel Prescot, was sent for that purpose ; but by some mistake, they proceeded to another high piece of ground, called Breed's hill, where they formed an entrenchment, before the dawn of day, undiscovered by the English ships, which lay quite near to them. As soon as the enemy saw this new work, they commenced a heavy cannonade upon it ; but this did not prevent the Americans from continuing their labour. As this hill overlooked Boston, General Gage thought it necessary to drive the Americans from it ; and for that purpose, he sent a detachment of about three thousand troops, commanded by General Howe. Two American

generals, Warren and Pomeroy, joined their
countrymen with as many more troops as made
their number amount to fifteen hundred. The
English advanced to attack the Americans on
the 17th of June, and while they were doing
so, their general gave orders that Charlestown
should be set on fire ; it contained about five
hundred houses, which were chiefly of wood ;
—the flames spread rapidly, so that in a short
time, the whole town formed one great blaze.
The inhabitants of Boston and the surrounding country were gazing on this awfully interesting scene, with anxious feelings for their
countrymen on Breed's hill. The English
troops advanced to within a hundred yards of
them, before the Americans fired ; and when
they did so, the English fell back. By the exertions of their officers, they were again led forward, but a second time were driven back.
A third time they were led up, and assisted by
the firing from the ships and floating batteries,
they attacked the Americans in three different
directions, and almost battered down their
works of defence. They had endeavoured to
increase their security by taking the rails from
the fences, and putting them in two rows, at a
short distance from each other, and then fill-
ing the space between with hay. Their ammunition was soon spent, and finding that it
would be vain to attempt longer to resist their
powerful foes, they retreated from the hill,
but claimed the victory, because they had lost

less than one half of the number which the British had lost in their attack. There is so much cause for sorrow connected with a victory in battle, that to a reflecting mind, there is no gladness in the sound; and English and Americans had reason to lament that sad disposition of nature "whence come wars and fightings," and which can only be restrained by that "wisdom which descendeth from above, and is full of mercy, peaceable, gentle, and easy to be entreated."

Thus fully began that dreadful conflict which for years was to desolate one of the finest portions of the globe. By it thousands lost their lives, and tens of thousands were involved in misery. But the hand of oppression was beginning to bind down the liberties of a grow ing nation—and through this mighty evil the great Ruler of events has brought forth the present prosperous state of our country.

Congress assembled May 10th, 1775. Peyton Randolph was chosen president. Being, however, under the necessity of returning home in a few days, John Hancock succeeded him.

Resistance to the oppressive measures of the British government was no longer a matter of doubt, and while petitions were coming in from all quarters urging the adoption of decisive measures, Congress was diligently preparing to sustain the rights of the colonies. When it was determined to organize an army, the eyes of all were directed to Washington as the commander-in-chief; and on the 15th of June, 1775, he was unanimously appointed to that post. The firmness of his temper, the dignity of his manners, and the confidence which was felt in his integrity and patriotism, made this choice by Congress satisfactory to all the people. When his appointment was made known to him, he modestly replied, " Mr. President, Though I am truly sensible of the honour done me in this appointment, yet I feel great distress, from a consciousness that my abilities and military experience may not be equal to the extensive and important trust; however, as the Congress desire it, I will enter upon the momentous duty, and exert every power I possess in their service, and for the support of the glorious cause. I beg they will accept my most cordial thanks for this distinguished testimony of their approbation.

" But lest some unlucky event should happen unfavourable to my reputation, I beg it may be remembered by every gentleman in the room, that I this day declare with the utmost sincerity, I do not think myself equal to the command I am honoured with.

" As to pay, sir, I beg leave to assure Congress that as no pecuniary consideration could have tempted me to accept this arduous employment, at the expense of my domestic ease and happiness, I do not wish to make any profit from it. I will keep an exact account of my expenses. Those I doubt not they will discharge, and that is all I desire."

The peaceful enjoyments of his comfortable home were to be given up, but no selfish desire of ease ever caused him to shrink from the performance of a duty which was to benefit others. It was the wish of his countrymen that he should accept this important part of the arduous work they expected to be engaged in; and he did so, with an earnest desire not to disappoint their confidence, and an humble trust that he should have the blessing of God on his efforts to do well for his country. He would not have drawn his sword to gain the name of conqueror, and he was willing to bear that of a soldier only when by doing so, he could defend the helpless, or aid in obtaining justice for the oppressed. What he had been to his native province, in his youth, he was to be to his country, in the strength of his manhood. Being a patriot in all his feelings, he informed Congress that he would not consent to receive any compensation for his services, but that he would keep an account of his expenses, which they might defray. He bade his family farewell, and set off for Cambridge, in Massachusetts, which was the place appointed as the headquarters of the army. On the way he received from the people constant proofs of the satisfaction which his appointment gave. In Massachusetts he was met with affectionate attention, and was welcomed by the army with

joy. He commenced immediately the difficult task of bringing the men into proper order. Their hands, which had been only used
to felling trees, striking the anvil, guiding the
plough, or to other peaceful and useful employments, could not readily handle well a
musket or a sword. They knew nothing of
the discipline that was needful to make them
useful as soldiers. They were fully resolved
to defend their rights, but this spirit of freedom
caused them to wish to do so in their own
way, and as they were not willing to submit
to rules and directions, the patience of their
commander was therefore severely tried. He
had naturally a very strong temper, but in his
boyhood he had determined to watch and sub-
due it. When any occurrence raised his anger, he resolutely endeavoured to restrain it,
and thus obeyed the Scripture precept given
to warm tempers, " Be ye angry and sin not."
He knew that he could not command others
so as to have their respect, if by the indulgence of passion he proved that he could not
command himself. In addition to the difficulty of regulating the army, he had the anxiety
of knowing that they were very scantily supplied with powder and arms, as there was
very little powder in the country, and the inhabitants of the different provinces did not
wish to part with what they thought they
might want to use for their own particular de
fence. Washington was very anxious to con-

ceal this deficiency from the English generals, and used every means possible to do so.
His army was placed so as to blockade the
English troops, who were stationed on Bunker's hill, Roxbury Neck, and in Boston
Knowing as he did the difficulty there would
be in getting supplies for his men, he wished
to make an attempt to drive the enemy from
Boston at once ; but his officers, on being
consulted, were of the opinion that the attempt
would not be successful, and the two armies
continued in the same situation for several
months.

As it was known that the English were endeavouring to engage the inhabitants of Canada, and the Indians, to assist them in invading
the provinces from that part of the country,
Congress sent troops there, who took possession of several forts. Washington resolved to
send a detachment from his army to Quebec,
and he gave the command of it to Colonel Arnold. The orders given to him were, to pass
through the country, not as an enemy to the
inhabitants of Canada, but as friends, and to
check with severity every attempt to injure
them ; and to treat with respect their religious
ceremonies : for, said Washington, " while
we are contending for our own liberty, we
should be very cautious of violating the rights
of conscience in others, and should ever consider, with a true Christian spirit, that God
alone is the judge of the hearts of men, and

to him only in this case are they answerable."
Arnold and his troops were thirty-two days
passing through a frightful wilderness, without seeing a house or a human being; they
waded through swamps and toiled over mountains, and arrived at Quebec worn down with
fatigue. Arnold expected to take Quebec by
surprise, but information had been given of
his approach, so that he was disappointed.
General Montgomery, who had taken Mon-
treal from the English, marched to join Arnold, and then endeavoured to prevail on the
commander of Quebec to give it up without
blood being shed; but the officer he sent with
a flag of truce was fired on, and he then determined on attacking the town. The attack
was bold but not successful, and in making it,
the brave Montgomery lost his life. The
blockade of Quebec was continued for some-
time without effect, and, on hearing that an
English fleet had arrived, the American officers concluded that it would be vain to expect
success, and gave up the siege. Several engagements convinced the Americans that their
force was not sufficient to accomplish in Canada what they had expected; and the officers
determined on retreating from it, before their
men should be more reduced by unavailing
sufferings.

At the time of these occurrences in the
north, the southern provinces were not quiet.
The governor of Virginia, assisted by ships

of war, attempted to burn the town of Hampton, but he was prevented by the bravery of the people. He then collected his force at Norfolk. An American regiment of regulars, and two hundred minute men, marched for the defence of that place; they were attacked by the English, whom they soon forced to retreat, with the loss of many of their number, though the Americans did not lose one man. The governor took refuge on board of a vessel; and on the night of the first of January, 1776, a heavy cannonade was commenced on the town from the ships, and some of the troops landed and set fire to the houses. As the Americans did not think that they could keep possession of Norfolk against the force of an English fleet, they made no efforts to extinguish the flames, but suffered them to rage until the town was consumed. After this the governor continued sailing up the rivers of Virginia for some time, burning houses and destroying plantations. A number of the inhabitants of the frontiers of the southern provinces, were inclined to favour the English, and formed themselves into companies; but they were met by the provincial parties, and obliged to fly in every direction. The governor of North Carolina had gone aboard of a ship of war in the Cape Fear river. General Clinton, who was to command the English in the south, arrived in North Carolina, with a small force; but he did not think it prudent

to use it there, and determined on going to
Charleston, in South Carolina. This intention was discovered, and all ranks of citizens
began immediately to prepare for defence. A
new fort, afterwards called Fort Moultrie, in
honour of its commander, was quickly built
on Sullivan's Island, which is at the mouth
of the harbour. In the beginning of June,
the British fleet anchored off the harbour of
Charleston. Some American troops arrived
from Virginia and North Carolina, and they
were all commanded by General Lee. The
streets of the city were barricaded; store-
houses of great value were pulled down, and
every possible means for defence were prepared. The English fleet was commanded by
Sir Peter Parker, and consisted of two-fifty-
gun ships, four frigates, and four smaller armed
vessels. On the 28th of June, they commenced
firing on Fort Moultrie, at about 10 o'clock in
the morning and continued to do so for three
hours; but the firing was returned from the
fort with so much skill, that the ships were
almost torn to pieces, and about 9 o'clock,
with difficulty were moved off. The loss of
the British in killed and wounded, exceeded
two hundred; while that of the Americans
was only ten killed and twenty-two wounded.

Thus did a feeble force of 375 regulars,
and a few militia, in a half-finished fort, crip-
ple and drive off, with little loss to themselves
a powerful and well commanded fleet. Truly

they had cause to use the language of the devout Asa, and say, " Lord, it is nothing with thee to help, whether with many, or with them that have no power." A few days afterwards, all the English troops who had been landed, returned to the vessels, and the whole fleet sailed away for New York, and the state of South Carolina was, for that time, delivered from the ravages of a foreign army.

This success, so providentially given the Americans in the south, encouraged them greatly, and cheered the anxious mind of Washington, when he was distressed by the unfavourable accounts from the north. His army had been very much changed during the winter; many of the men had returned to their homes, and new recruits had taken their places ; so that he was constantly obliged to bear the trial of patience in his endeavour to have a regular force. He was still of opinion, that an attempt to drive the enemy from Boston would be successful ; in writing to Congress on the subject, he said, " I cannot help acknowledging, that I have many disagreeable sensations on account of my situation ; for to have the eyes of the whole continent fixed on me, with anxious expectation of hearing of some great event, and to be restrained in every military operation, for want of the necessary means to carry it on, is not very pleasing ; especially as the means used to conceal my weakness from the enemy conceal it also from our friends, and add to their wonder."

Towards the latter end of February, having received a fresh supply of powder, he resolved on attempting to force General Howe from Boston, and commenced an attack early in March; a considerable detachment of Americans took possession of the heights of Dorchester, and in one night, though the ground was frozen, raised works, which in a great degree covered them from the shot of the enemy. It was then necessary for the English, either to drive the Americans from those heights, or to leave the town; the former was determined on, and troops were put on board of the ships to proceed down the bay for that purpose. They were not, however, allowed by " Him who ruleth the winds and the waves," to succeed, for they were scattered by a violent storm, and entirely disabled from proceeding; and before they could be ready again to make the attempt, the Americans had made their works of defence so strong, that it was thought useless to try to force them. In expectation that most of the troops would be engaged in this attack, General Washington had made preparations for attacking those that remained in Boston; but this plan was disappointed by the English general determining on leaving it, when he saw the Dorchester heights could not be taken. When General Washington knew of the intentions

of General Howe, he thought it most probable that he would go from Boston to New
York, and he sent a large portion of his army
there immediately.

On the 17th of March, the English entered
their ships, and soon the whole fleet sailed;
the rest of the American army then marched
to New York. The recovery of Boston caused
great joy. When Washington entered it, he
was received by the inhabitants as their deli-
verer from oppression; and in their public
address to him, they expressed the wish, " May
you still go on, approved by Heaven, and revered by all good men." The fleet sailed to
Halifax, and remained there until June, and
then left it, and early in July landed the troops
on Staten Island.

CHAPTER III.

1776—1777.

WHEN the war commenced, the Americans thought only of obtaining relief from
the oppression of unjust laws; but when
they heard that the English had hired foreign troops to assist in subduing them, and
had engaged the tomahawk of the Indian
against them, they began to think of an
entire separation from England, and of de-

claring themselves to be an independent people. A few bold ones, at first, spoke of this;
and then it was soon openly talked of through
out all the provinces. Several of the provincial
assemblies gave an opinion in favour of it, and
on the 7th of June, 1776, it was proposed in
Congress by Richard Henry Lee, and seconded by John Adams. The resolution was in
these words: " Resolved, that these United
Colonies are, and of right ought to be, free
and independent states ; and that all political
connexion between them and the state of Great
Britain is, and ought to be totally dissolved."
Congress, at that time, held their meetings in
the State-House, at Philadelphia, and the room
in which they sat has ever since been called
" Independence Hall."

After much serious deliberation, the thirteen Colonies at length agreed, through their
representatives, to the resolution, and it was
adopted by Congress on the 2d of July. On
that day, the Declaration of Independence was
proposed by the committee who had been in
structed to prepare it,* and, after a debate of
three days, during which several amendments

* The Declaration was written by Mr. Jefferson, after
wards President of the United States. The motion to authorize the Declaration was, as we have seen, seconded by
Mr. John Adams, who also was afterwards President· Both
of these eminent patriots died on the *fourth of July*, 1826,
exactly half a century from the day on which they put their
names to the paper. [See appendix **A.**]

were made, it was agreed to on the 4th of July and signed by every member then present, excepting one, who thought that it was too soon to take such a step. Among the amendments made by Congress to the original draft of the declaration, was the inserting of the words—" With a firm reliance on the protec-tion of Divine Providence," in the last sentence declaring that " for the support of this declaration we mutually pledge to each other our lives, our fortunes, and our sacred ho-nour." Thus we see that this distinguished body of men were anxious to acknowledge in a document, which is the most important in the history of our country, that they were dependent on the blessing of God for success in their undertaking. This declaration was first written and signed on paper, but was afterwards copied on parchment, and signed again on the 2d of August. Several persons signed it then who were not members of Congress on the 4th of July, and some, being absent at the time, did not put their names to it until October.* There are fifty-six signatures to the parchment copy, which is now kept in the public offices at Washington. So great is the estimation in which those persons are held who signed this paper, that an account of the life of each of them has been published, and the document is held in the highest veneration by every American. The yearly return of the important day on which it was signed, has

* See appendix (B)

ever since been hailed with gladness. And so
it should be; but not with the riotous joy
which disregards the laws of God and man
Temperate and harmless recreation should be
mingled with grateful acknowledgments of the
goodness of that all-powerful and all-merciful
Being, who gave us such cause for gladness.

No longer striving for the repeal of objec-
tionable laws, but for their existence as a nation, the people were united and vigorous, and
a new impulse was felt throughout the STATES,
now no longer colonies. All men had now to
take sides, either for or against their country,
and the voice of the people was nearly one for
liberty and independence.

About the time at which Independence was
declared, the brother of General Howe arrived
at Staten Island, with a large fleet, and a number of troops. General Washington had made
every preparation in his power for defending
New York; but was soon convinced that he
could not prevent the English ships from passing up the Hudson river. While he was thus
anxiously engaged, letters were sent from the
commander of the fleet, addressed to the governors under the king; requesting them to
make known to the people that he had authority from the king to grant pardons to all those
who would return to their duty; and that
every person who would aid in persuading
them to do so, should be rewarded. General
Washington sent these papers immediately to

Congress, who resolved to publish them. A the same time, General Howe sent an officer on shore, with a flag of truce, and a letter ad dressed to " George Washington, Esquire.' He refused to receive it, as he considered it a disrespect to his countrymen, who had given him the title of " Commander-in-chief " of their armies. Another letter was sent, direct- ed to George Washington, &c. &c. &c., and the officer who brought it said that the addi- tion of &c. &c. &c. meant every thing that ought to follow the name. General Washing- ton said they meant every thing, it was true, but they also might mean any thing ; and he should refuse to receive a letter on public bu- siness, if it was directed to him as a private person. The officer assured him that no dis- respect was intended, and that General Howe and his brother had been appointed by the king of England to " settle the unhappy dis- pute which had arisen." Washington told him that he had no power from Congress to say any thing on that subject; but, from what he could learn, it was his opinion that Gen. Howe and his brother were only to grant pardons, and " those who had committed no fault, wanted no pardon: the Americans were only defending what they considered their just rights."

The English army consisted of about twen- ty-four thousand men, and was abundantly supplied with military stores, and a numerous fleet was ready to aid it. The American army, of about thirteen thousand men, for three different situations, was scantily furnished with arms ; and Washington, after giving an account of its state to Congress, added ; "These things are melancholy, but nevertheless true. I hope for better. Under every disadvantage, my utmost exertions shall be employed to bring about the great end we have in view. As far as I can judge, from the apparent dispositions of my troops, I shall have their support. The superiority of the enemy, and the expected attack, do not seem to have affected their spirits." A part of the army was on Long Island, the rest on York and Governor's Islands, and Paules-hook. Washington earnestly endeavoured to encourage his troops ; he said, " the time is perhaps near at hand, which will probably determine whether Americans are to be freemen. The fate of unknown millions will depend, under God, on the courage and conduct of this army. Let us rely on the goodness of our cause, and the aid of the Supreme Being, in whose hands victory is, to animate and encourage us to great and noble actions."

General Howe landed his troops on Long Island on the 22d July, and the Americans prepared for being attacked ; a detachment of them, which had been stationed to give notice of the approach of the enemy, was surrounded and seized ; and this gave an opportunity to

the English of advancing by a way that was
very favourable for their attack,—which was
made with so large a force, and in so many
different directions, that it was not in the
power of the Americans to resist with success,
though they did so with bravery.   General
Washington passed over to Brooklyn, and
saw, with deep sorrow, the destruction of his
troops.   He had no power to aid them in any
other way than by his own exertions ; for he
saw, that if he brought over the rest of his
troops from New York, the superior force of
the enemy would overpower them all, and
thus the fate of his country be at once decided.
The English encamped in front of the remaining Americans, and Washington determined
on endeavouring to save them by withdrawing
them from Long Island.   He formed his plan,
and when the night of the twenty-eighth
came, under his directions, and assisted by
his exertions, all the troops and military
stores, with a great part of the provisions,
and all the artillery, were carried over to
New York in safety.   A kind Providence favoured the Americans with a night so dark
and a morning so foggy, that though their
enemies were within a few hundred yards of
them, they did not know of the movement
they were making, until they were beyond the
reach of their guns. From the commencement
of the action, on the morning of the 27th of
July, until the troops had crossed safely, on

the 29th, their anxious commander had not closed his eyes; and was almost all the time on horseback, directing and aiding them. He did not think of his own preservation until the last boat was leaving the shore, and he then placed himself in it, with a sad heart.

This event discouraged the American army so much, that, as General Washington wrote to Congress, their situation was "truly distressing," and he had to suffer the pain of seeing whole regiments return in despair to their homes.

The first use which General Howe made of his success, was to send a message to Philadelphia, that though he could not treat with Congress as a body, he had full power to settle the controversy upon terms that would be very favourable ; and that he would meet any of the members in their private character, at any place they would appoint. Congress informed him, that being the representatives of a free and independent people, they could not send any of their members to speak with him in their private character ; but that, being desirous of peace, they would send a committee to understand from him what offers he was permitted to make. Three members, Benjamin Franklin, John Adams, and Edward Rutledge, were appointed by Congress to visit Staten Island, where they were very civilly received by the English commander, but as any proposal he had to make was only on

condition of the colonies returning to obedience, which was not listened to, the matter
dropped here.

From the movements of the English army
and fleet, General Washington found that it
was their intention to surround New York,
and force him into a battle. The depressed
state of his army convinced him that this
would be destructive to his troops, and he
thought it would be right to withdraw them
from New York. In writing to Congress he
said, "On every side there is a choice of difficulties. * * On our part the war should be
defensive; we should, on all occasions, avoid
a general action; nor put any thing to the risk,
unless compelled by necessity, into which we
ought never to be drawn."

On consulting together, the officers of the
army agreed, that it was best to give up New
York, and Washington employed himself actively in removing the military stores to a
place of safety. He had urged the inhabitants to
remove the women and children from it when
the enemy first appeared on Staten Island.

When the American troops were withdrawn
from New York, they were stationed at Kings
bridge, and the enemy took possession of the
city on the 15th September. The situation
of the American army was then very distressing to Washington; the time for which many
of the soldiers had agreed to serve was almost
spent, and he had but a faint expectation that

others would be soon engaged in their places. he wrote to Congress on the subject, urging them to make immediate endeavours to keep up the army. He commenced his letter in words which show his anxiety and modest faithfulness: " From the hours allotted to sleep, I will borrow a few moments to convey my thoughts on sundry important matters to Congress. I shall offer them with that sincerity which ought to characterize a man of candour, and with the freedom which may be used in giving useful information, without incurring the imputation of presumption." On receiving this long and very serious letter, Congress resolved to attend to the counsel which it contained, and appointed committees to make exertions for raising more troops.

General Howe wished to prevent the American army having intercourse with the New England states, and he marched his troops with an intention to surround the principal division of the army. But General Washington was too watchful to permit him to succeed in doing so. Several actions were fought by small detachments from each army, but he carefully avoided a general battle ; except in one instance, when he was favourably situated on the hills, near the White Plains, in the state of New York ; the English General declined it then, and changed his plans, and retired slowly down the North river, to enter New Jersey. When Washington discovered his intention, he wrote to the governor of that state, to inform him of it, and to General Green, who was placed there with some American troops; and he requested them to make every preparation possible for defence. He then placed all the troops that he could spare in the forts of the Highlands, in the state of New York; and passed over into New Jersey with his little army, in the middle of November. Cornwallis, an English general, followed with a large force, and Washington moved on to New Brunswick, where he stopped. There he had the mortification of seeing his army made still less, by the departure of many of the soldiers whose time had expired. He again wrote to the governor for some aid, but he had not the power to give it. He wrote urgently to General Lee, (who commanded the eastern troops,) to join him as quickly as possible. This sad situation brought into exercise all his wisdom and firmness. His army was reduced to about three thousand men; and they were scantily armed, poorly clad, and many of them barefooted. The army that pressed after them was more than double their number, well armed, well clad and fed, and in high spirits.

The contrast between the splendid appearance of the English, and the sad and ragged condition of the Americans, seemed to make the triumph of the former certain.

Afflicted, but not dismayed, by the cheer-

lessness of his prospects, Washington did not
cease for a moment to act with animation, and
encouraged his few troops with expressions
of confidence that they should not be delivered into the hands of their enemies. He remained at New Brunswick until they were in
sight, and then moved on towards the Delaware river, and soon succeeded in having the
military stores and scanty baggage of his army conveyed across, and the men who were
sick sent to Philadelphia.

The citizens determined to give all the aid
in their power to Washington, and fifteen
hundred of them marched immediately to join
him. He had sent twelve hundred men back
to Princeton, with the hope that by thus appearing to advance towards the enemy, he
might delay them, and give some encourage-
ment to the inhabitants of New Jersey. When
the troops from Philadelphia joined him, he
marched towards Princeton, but heard that
Cornwallis had received a large addition to
his troops, and was advancing by different roads to surround him. Again he was
obliged to retreat, and crossed the Delaware.
He secured all the boats, and broke down the
bridges on the roads along the Jersey shore,
and placed his army in such a manner as to
guard, as well as possible, all the fording
places.

As the last of the Americans crossed the
river, the English army appeared. The main

part of it was at Trenton, and detachments above and below, so as to make it quite uncertain where they intended to attempt crossing the river. Washington sent officers to Philadelphia, with directions to form lines of defence there, and to endeavour to secure the military stores. He gave particular orders on the 8th of December, to all the officers of his little army, to enable them to know how to act, in case the enemy attempted to cross the river. One of his officers said, with despondency, " How far must we go on retreating ?" " To Virginia," said Washington ; " and, if followed there, over the Alleghany Mountains, and try what we can do there."

General Lee advanced slowly with his troops, and imprudently slept at a distance of three miles from his army, in a farm house, at about twenty miles from the enemy. Information of this was given, and an English officer sent a company well mounted, who reached the farm house and surrounded it before General Lee had left it ; he was carried to the English army, and considered as a deserter from the British service. General Sullivan, the next in command to Lee, immediately hastened the march of the troops, and soon joined General Washington.

All the attempts of the English to get boats to cross the river failed, and their general determined to place them in quarters for the winter, which had commenced. Some were

placed in Princeton, and the rest at the principal towns of that part of New Jersey.

Washington thought that it was not probable Cornwallis would remain in winter shelter
longer than until the ice should be strong
enough for his troops to cross it, and he employed his anxious and active mind in reflect
ing on some plan for stopping the success of
the foes of his country. While they were
comfortably housed, the Americans were exposed to the wintry blasts ; for not many
could be sheltered in farm houses near enough
to each other; and those who could not, made
the frozen ground their bed and their knap-
sacks their pillows. No doubt many who thus
lay, offered fervent and humble prayers to
God, who suits his mercies to the necessities
of all who honour him ; and beneath the care
which he has promised to those who put their
trust in him, they slept soundly, though they
were unsheltered.

When General Washington reflected on the
dispersed situation of the English troops, he
said, " Now is the time to clip their wings,
when they are so spread." For this purpose
he formed a bold plan. He separated his army into three divisions. One, consisting of
about two thousand four hundred men, commanded by himself, was to cross the Delaware, at M'Konky's Ferry, about nine miles
above Trenton, and then to march down in
two divisions ; one taking the river road, and

the other the Pennington road, both of which led into the town; the one at the west end, and the other towards the north. The second division of the army, commanded by General Irvine, was to cross at Trenton Ferry, and secure the bridge below the town, so as to prevent the enemy from escaping by that way. The third, commanded by General Cadwalader, was to cross at Bristol, and make an attack on the troops posted at Burlington.

Christmas night was appointed for the different divisions to cross the river. As the night approached, a driving sleet fell, and the cold became severe. Washington, with the division which he commanded, was the greater part of the night struggling amidst the ice, which was driven in fearful wildness; rain and snow fell in a mingled shower, and it was four o'clock, on the morning of the 26th, before they succeeded in reaching the New Jersey shore. One division then marched, as had been planned, by the river road, and the other by the Pennington road. Washington arrived at Trenton exactly at eight o'clock, and drove in the outguards of the enemy, and in three minutes he heard the other division doing the same.

Colonel Rawlè, the English commander, paraded his troops to meet the Americans, but he was soon mortally wounded, and his troops then attempted to move off. Washington sent a detachment to meet them as they were retreating, and the enemy finding themselves surrounded, laid down their arms.

The divisions of the American army which were commanded by Generals Irvine and Cadwalader, had not been able to cross the river amid the driving ice; and as that part of the plan which they were to perform failed Washington concluded it would not be prudent to remain with his small force where he should probably be soon attacked by the collected force of his enemies; he therefore recrossed the Delaware with his prisoners, and military stores that he had taken. One thousand was the number of the prisoners. Two American soldiers had been killed, and two or three wounded, and one officer.

This bold and successful attack occasioned great astonishment to the English army, as they had believed the Americans to be in a state too feeble to attempt resistance, even when it should suit their enemies to leave their comfortable quarters to attack them.

Cornwallis had gone to New York, but he returned immediately to New Jersey, with more troops, to regain the ground which had been thus unexpectedly taken from him. The officer who commanded at Burlington, marched his troops to Princeton, and the division of the American army which was opposite, crossed over and took possession of Burlington.

Washington resolved not to remain idle,

and he passed again over to Trenton, to endeavour to recover at least a part of New Jersey. The English collected in full force at Princeton, and formed there some works of defence. Washington collected all his troops together at Trenton, and the next day the English army approached it. He then crossed the Assumpinck creek, which runs through the town, and drew up his army beside it. The enemy attempted to cross it, but were prevented, and they halted and kindled their night fires.

The situation of Washington was a very dangerous one. If he remained as he was, he was almost sure of being attacked, at the dawn of day, by a force far superior to his own; and he thought that the destruction of his little army must be the consequence. To pass the Delaware was almost impossible, from the state it was in, with masses of drifting ice. Wisdom to plan, and strength to act, were given to him by the mighty God of armies.

The night fires of the English burned brightly, and Washington directed his troops to light their fires along the edge of the creek. The bright close blaze became as a screening cloud between their enemies and them, while it was as a pillar of fire to light them in the silent preparations which their commander directed them to make for moving away.

That important night was particularly

marked by the favour of Divine Providence:
and in after years, many a pious father, seated
in his comfortable home, and surrounded by
the children for whose rights he had that
night been struggling, delighted, with devout
thankfulness, to tell them, how the clouds
and the winds were commanded by their
great Ruler, to aid a people struggling for
their liberty.

Several days of soft weather had made the
roads very deep; a light rain had been falling,
but suddenly the clouds were driven off by a
strong west wind, which was so cold that
the roads were frozen by it, and became like
a pavement, over which Washington and his
little army moved in silence, towards Princeton, and arrived within a short distance of it,
early in the morning.

Three British regiments had encamped at
Princeton the preceding night. A small party,
at the distance of more than a mile, discovered
the arms of the Americans glittering in the
beams of the rising sun; they immediately
returned to their camp, gave the alarm, and
prevented a complete surprise. The British
advanced towards the Americans, and attacked
the militia, who were in front; they gave way,
and General Mercer, a very valuable officer
from Virginia, was killed while he was endeavouring to rally the broken troops. Washington feeling assured that a defeat then would
be ruinous to the interest of his country, rode

forward with speed, placed himself between the enemy and his own troops, and by his commands and example restored them to order. He was between the fires of the two armies, but the protecting shield of his Creator was again on every side, to preserve him from the weapons of destruction. He entered Princeton, and after a short action, took possession of it, and secured three hundred prisoners. A part of the British troops took refuge in the College, but were soon forced to surrender by the fire of the Americans.

After the action, a militia officer, (who never turned away from the complaints of a suffering fellow-being, whether friend or foe,) in passing where some dead bodies were stretched, heard a moan; he stopped to listen, and in a few moments discovered the wounded sufferer who uttered it. He raised him tenderly in his arms, and asked if he could relieve him; the wounded man, faintly said, " No, it is too late," and then made an effort to speak his own name, and that of an English officer, and added, " Take my watch, and send it to him; take my razor from my knapsack, and keep it, as the gift of a grateful, dying man." His eyes closed in death, and his request was faithfully performed. His gift was kept with care, and in after days, shown by its owner, with a satisfactory recollection of the confidence of a dying enemy.

The same officer, in writing to his family

an account of the battle at Princeton, said,
' I would wish to say a few words respecting
the actions of that truly great man, General
Washington, but it is not in my power to convey any just ideas of him. I shall never forget what I felt when I saw him brave all the
dangers of the field, his important life hanging as it were by a single hair, with a thousand deaths flying around him. I thought
not of myself. He is surely Heaven's pecu-
liar care."

The British troops at Trenton were under
arms, and about to attack the Americans by
the light of the dawn ; but when it came, they
discovered that the whole force, with their
baggage and stores, had withdrawn; and they
soon heard the sound of their cannon at
Princeton, which, though in the midst of winter, they supposed to be thunder.

Again was Washington surrounded with
perplexing perils. His wearied troops had
been one night, and some of them two, with
out sleep. The march had been fatiguing
and painful to the soldiers, whose bare feet
left traces of blood to mark their path, and
the cold was piercing to those who were
thinly clad. Fearing an attack in this condition from the English army, which was so
much larger, and not wearied by fatiguing
marches and loss of rest, he gave up his plan
of going to New-Brunswick; and breaking
down all the bridges over the creeks between

that place and Princeton, he moved to Pluck-
emin, where his troops rested.   Cornwallis,
alarmed by the events at Trenton and Princeton, marched to New-Brunswick, and began
to move his military stores to a place of
greater safety.

The suffering state of the Americans from
want of tents, clothes, and blankets, induced
their commander to determine on putting them
under shelter for the rest of the winter ; and
he marched for this purpose to Morristown.

The ranks of the American army had often
been thinned by that dreadful disease, the
small pox.   The blessing of vaccination was
not then known; and inoculation had seldom
been practised in this country. General Washington formed the bold, but judicious resolution, of having every officer and soldier who
had not had the disease, inoculated.   This
was done very successfully, and the troops
being undisturbed during the progress of the
complaint, recovered under the care of Him
who healeth all our diseases.

The unexpected and successful attacks
made at Trenton and Princeton, by an army
that was thought to be conquered, saved Philadelphia for that winter ; and revived the
spirits of the Americans so much, that the
difficulty of raising troops for the next season,
was lessened in all the states.

In compliance with the advice of Washington, Congress had resolved to enlist sol-

diers who would consent to serve while the war continued. This was very satisfactory to him; as he had suffered much from the short enlistments, by which his army had often been reduced when he most needed a strong force. When the American army had retreated through New-Jersey, the inhabitants were so sure of its destruction, that they thought it would be useless to make any attempt to defend themselves; but after the successful engagements at Trenton and Princeton, they were so cheered, that they collected in large companies, and the militia became very active in assisting to confine the English to Amboy and New-Brunswick, where they were stationed when Washington led his army to Morristown.

Through this period of universal depression, Congress had acted with firmness, and an unchanged resolution to trust the event of the contest to Divine Providence, and adhere to the Independence they had declared. Supposing that the enemy would advance to Philadelphia, they removed to Baltimore, and made efforts to encourage their countrymen, and lead them to persist in what seemed to be an almost hopeless cause. They advised each state to appoint a day of humiliation and prayer, to implore God to forgive their sins as a people, and assist them by his favour in their day of trouble. And they soon had reason to praise him for giving them cause to

feel, that " though cast down," they were
" not forsaken." During that season of deepest gloom which had overspread the United
States, when the hearts of all were tried, he
who bore the greatest responsibility, felt most
keenly for the fate of his country. The
late Governor Brooks, of Massachusetts, then
an Aid to Washington, came to him from a
tour of duty, in his own state. He found the
General deeply affected, and as he talked of
the condition of his troops, and the wrongs of
his country, he shed tears of grief. " Sir,"
said he, " my only hope is in God. Go back
to Massachusetts, and do what you can to
raise men and money." Thus felt and spoke
the man, whom nations admire, and who was
sensible that there is a God in heaven, who
rules not there alone, but also among the
children of men. His confidence was not in
vain. From the midst of darkness came a
light that cheered the hearts of his countrymen, and the drooping spirits of the nation
were revived.

While the Americans were in Morristown,
their number was so small, that it was difficult for Washington to keep up the appearance
of an army ; but he sent out small detachments to show themselves in different directions ; and with the assistance of the New-
Jersey militia, succeeded in keeping the enemy from again overspreading the country.
As the spring advanced, and new troops were

raised, there was a difficulty in assembling them as the commander-in-chief wished; for the English had possession of the ocean, and so could attack any state in the union; and each one desired to be defended. This could not be done, without separating the troops into small divisions, and placing them distant from each other. Washington possessed that solid judgment which makes the best use of small means; and he determined to prepare in the surest manner that could be effected for defending the eastern states, the highlands of New York, where it was very important to preserve the forts, and Philadelphia, which seemed to be the object of Cornwallis. When he had placed troops for this purpose, he formed his own camp at Middlebrook, in New Jersey, with not quite six thousand men.

Early in June, the English army was increased by troops from New York, and the commander moved them in different directions, for the purpose of drawing Washington from his camp to a battle; but he was too wise to be led into danger, which would have been almost certain destruction to his small army. He continued watching the movements of the enemy with anxiety. Sometimes they appeared as if intending to go to the north, and then moved towards the south. Washington kept his troops posted on the heights, in front of his camp, always ready in case of an attack. He wrote to General Arnold his opinion, that it was the intention of the enemy to destroy his army, and get possession of Philadelphia, but that he would endeavour to prevent the first part of the plan being successful; and if they moved towards Philadelphia, he would be close after them to do every thing in his power to delay them.

The English commander, finding that he could not draw Washington from his camp, determined on removing to New Jersey, and taking them on board of the fleet to the Chesapeake or Delaware. Washington took advantage of this, and moved his army for the purpose of following the enemy cautiously. They had passed over to Staten Island, but their commander suddenly resolved on returning to endeavour to get possession of the situation Washington had left, who immediately moved back, and prevented the success of this plan. The whole English army then crossed to Staten Island, and entered the fleet.

At that time, an English general named Prescot, commanded troops on Rhode Island; a militia officer, named Barton, with a small party, passed ten miles by water without being observed by the ships of war; and then landed within a mile of the place where they knew General Prescot slept. They quietly seized the guards, and took the general from his bed, and conveyed him in safety to their own quarters. The success of this bold attempt gave great joy; because it was expected

that the English would consent to give up
General Lee for General Prescot.

On receiving an account that the English
fleet had sailed from New York, the American
army was moved towards Philadelphia.

The English had a large force at Quebec,
commanded by General Burgoyne. Sir William Howe wrote to him, that though he
seemed to be moving towards the south, it
was his intention to turn towards Boston,
which he meant to attack, assisted by Burgoyne's troops. This letter was given to Gen.
Putnam, by a man who said he had been directed to take it to Quebec. Putnam sent it
immediately to General Washington. When
he read the letter, he said he was certain it
was written with the intention that it should
fall into his hands to deceive him ; and it convinced him that the enemy would soon be near
to Philadelphia ; but knowing that the American army in the north was a feeble one, he
proved the patriotism of his feelings by lessening his own force to assist them. The real
advantage of his countrymen, and not the ac-
quirement of fame for himself, was the mo-
tive which always ruled his actions as an officer.

He called out the militia of Maryland,
Pennsylvania, and the northern part of Virginia, and then marched with his own troops
towards the head of Elk river, in Maryland.

A militia officer, in writing to his family an

account of the appearance of the army as it passed through Philadelphia, said, "As Washington, the most dignified and respectable of mortals, marching at the head of the American army, passed, the tories hid their heads and trembled, whilst the friends of freedom appeared on each side of the streets, and bowed with gratitude and respect to the great man; and were I to judge of his feelings, I think he would not have exchanged his situation for all that kings in their profusion could bestow."

As Washington advanced towards Elk river, he heard that the enemy were landing, whose whole force consisted of about eighteen thousand men, in good health, high spirits, and well trained.   Washington's force was about eleven thousand, and not all of these were supplied with arms.

He was desirous to place his army in the most favourable situation for meeting their powerful foes, and he moved to the Brandywine Creek, in the state of Delaware, and took possession of the high grounds, extending southward from Chad's Ford.   He knew that Philadelphia could not be saved without a successful battle;   and that Congress, and the people generally, expected that he would not give it up without an attempt to prevent the enemy from possessing it. In making his preparations for an attack, he was deceived by a false account of the number of the enemy and of their movements as they were advancing and was therefore disappointed in the most important part of the plan he had formed for meeting them. When they drew near, he used great efforts to encourage his troops, and on the 11th of September an action com-menced, which was very severe. Sir William Howe was successful in driving the Americans from the ground, but they were not too much discouraged to risk another action for the safety of Philadelphia.

Washington allowed them one day for rest, and then marched on the Lancaster road, to a spot near the Warren Tavern, about twenty-three miles from Philadelphia. In a few hours he heard that the enemy were approaching, and he prepared to meet them. The dreadful work of destruction was commencing, when a powerful rain began to fall, and became so violent that the arms of the Americans were soon unfit for use; a retreat was absolutely necessary, and as Washington was convinced that his army was not in a state to gain success in an action, he determined to avoid being attacked. He directed that all the military stores in the city should be removed to a place of safety, so that very little public property might fall into the hands of the enemy, who, headed by Cornwallis, entered Philadelphia on the 26th of September.

Congress separated on the 18th September, and met at Lancaster, in Pennsylvania on the 27th. Washington took a position beyond Germantown, that he might attack the British troops posted at that village. On the 30th October an assault was made, but a heavy fog and darkness caused mistakes in the movements of the troops, and a skilful retreat was all that the commander could effect, and for his management of this, he received the thanks of Congress. The chief point of contest was at Chew's house, in the upper part of Germantown, which still bears the marks of the battle.

The news of this attack on the enemy, although unsuccessful, made a great impression in our favour in Europe, and military men began to believe that such skill and valour would be finally successful. The loss of American soldiers and officers was much greater than that of the British, but they lost also some valuable officers. One of these was attended in a house in Germantown, by a female, who endeavoured to give some relief to his sufferings; but he felt that all human aid was vain, and said, " *Woman pray for me.*" Thus in that hour, when the soul feels what it truly is, and that soon it must be in the presence of its holy Creator and just Judge, the duty and the value of *prayer* is owned; and on almost every bed of death is fulfilled the words of Scripture, " O Thou that hearest prayer, unto Thee shall all flesh come."

Soon after the battle of Germantown, Sir

William Howe drew all his troops into Philadelphia, to employ them in removing the obstructions which had been placed in the Delaware river, to prevent his ships from passing up to the city. Washington had placed troops in Fort Mifflin, on Mud Island, and in a redoubt a few miles from Philadelphia, at Red Bank, a high bluff, so called from the colour of the sand on it. Count Donop, a German officer, was sent with a detachment of Hessians of about twelve hundred men, to at tack the fort at Red Bank, which was commanded by Colonel Greene. On the evening of the 22d of October, Donop appeared before the fort; Greene, with his garrison of five hundred men, received him bravely ; and the assault and defence were both spirited and obstinate. Donop was killed, and the second in command, Colonel Wingerode, fell at the same time ; the oldest remaining officer then drew off his troops, and returned to Philadelphia. The loss of the assailants was four hundred, and of the defenders, thirty-two killed and wounded. A continued struggle was kept up for more than six weeks, to prevent the English in Philadelphia having free communication with their fleet, but at length they succeeded.

Several officers had been wounded at the battle of Brandywine, and among these was the marquis Lafayette. This generous stranger was early called to bleed in that cause for which he had ventured his all. He had left France, his native land, and come to America to risk his life and spend his fortune in the cause of liberty. He was only nineteen years of age, when he gave up a gay scene of youthful pleasures to enter on one of dangerous toils. The American commissioners who were in France honestly told him of the depressed state of the American army, and of the sufferings that he would be exposed to. This did not change, but fixed his generous intention, and he hastened his preparations to cross the ocean, and make known to Congress his purpose, and arrived in Charleston early in the year 1777. They welcomed with respect this brave friend of their country, and gave him the commission of a major-general in their army; a title which he has ever since preferred to that of marquis. His disinterested conduct, and amiable character, made Washington his friend: and he could not know and be near to Washington without becoming attached to him. Their friendship was sincere, warm, and steady.

Thus, in his first visit to our country, Lafayette was welcomed as a friend to the cause of liberty; and his determination to share in the toils and dangers of the Americans, in their struggle to obtain it, was as lasting as it was ardent, and not like the bright morning cloud which soon passes away. And when, in August of the year 1824, he again visited our country, to behold the prosperity with which the God of nations has blessed it, the joyful and grateful manner in which he was received throughout the United States, proved that Americans had not forgotten his generous services.   Old soldiers grasped his friendly hand with a welcome of affectionate gladness; children, in thousands, pressed around him to share the kind notice of his eye; and all the people were of one mind in desiring to show him some mark of grateful respect.   In accordance with this general feeling, Congress bestowed on him a tract of land constituting a township in the state of Alabama, and fifty thousand dollars in money.   They invited him to make the United States his home, but his own country was still under an oppressive government, and he returned to promote the cause of liberty there.   His conduct in the revolution of 1830, when Charles X., King of France, was driven from the throne and country, contributed greatly to restrain the violence of the people, and to avert the horrors of a civil war.

CHAPTER IV.

1777.

WHILE Washington kept up the contest in the middle states, very interesting events were passing in the northern states.

A plan had been formed by the British government, for sending an army to pass from Canada to the Hudson river, by the way of the lakes, and to take possession of all the American forts. General Burgoyne had the command of this army, and he engaged several Indian warriors, who thirsted for blood and plunder, to join him. A fleet was ready on the lakes to assist him. When these preparations were known, the people were filled with terror; the fear of the tomahawk and scalping-knife added greatly to their dread of the power of the English. General Burgoyne made a war-speech to his ferocious allies, the Indians; they listened attentively, but his charge to refrain from cruelty was not remembered, when they had the power to indulge man's violent dispositions.

Ticonderoga was commanded by General St. Clair. On the 1st of July Burgoyne prepared to attack the fort, and his force was so powerful and so well arranged that General St. Clair was convinced that resistance would ensure the destruction of all his troops, and he determined on withdrawing secretly. Orders were given to march out quietly, and set nothing on fire; but this order was not obeyed, and a house was soon in flames, which served as a signal to the enemy, who immediately entered the fort, and fired on the retreating troops, and then followed them and attacked them with so much ardour, that they were in a short time reduced to a very small number.

General Schuyler had been advancing from
Stillwater with troops, when he heard of the
retreat of St. Clair, and he then used great efforts to obtain a larger force, that he might
stop the progress of the enemy.   St. Clair
continued retreating, closely pursued, until at
length he joined General Schuyler, who had
returned with his troops to Stillwater.

When General Washington heard the sad
news from the north, he wrote to General
Schuyler, "This stroke is indeed severe;
but, notwithstanding things at present wear a
dark and gloomy aspect, I hope a spirited opposition will check the progress of General
Burgoyne's arms, and that the confidence derived from success will hurry him into measures that will in their consequences be favourable to us.   We should never despair
Our situation has been unpromising, and has
changed for the better.   So, I trust, it will
again.   If new difficulties arise, we must only
put forth new exertions."

After taking Ticonderoga, Burgoyne sent a
part of his army, up the lake, to Skeensbo-
rough, where they destroyed the American
flotilla, and a considerable quantity of military
stores.

The success of Burgoyne had the effect
which Washington had hoped for.   He was
so confident of conquering by his well ordered
troops, that he determined on dividing his
army, and sending detachments in different di-

rections, that he might overrun a larger portion of the country at once. He sent a detachment of five hundred English and one hundred Indians to seize the military stores at the town of Bennington, in Vermont. General Starke attacked and entirely routed these troops; the greater part of them were killed or taken prisoners; a few escaped into the woods. Other troops, sent by Burgoyne, arrived, and met their flying comrades. They were attacked by the Americans, and obliged to give up their baggage and artillery, and save themselves by retreating under cover of the night.

In this action the Americans gained one thousand stand of arms from the enemy, and the report of the British killed and wounded was seven hundred, and of Americans, one hundred.

These sanguinary battles are not recited to fill the mind with a love of scenes which should strike us with horror, at the dreadful result produced by human passions. They are facts, however, connected with our country's struggle for liberty; and, no doubt, such signal success encouraged greatly the hearts of those who stood up for its defence.

General Gates took the command of the northern army. General Washington had sent a detachment of riflemen from his own army, and had directed all the troops that were in Massachusetts to join them; and General Gates, with this force, met Burgoyne at

Stillwater, where a battle was fought on the 19th September, which was very severe, and neither army could claim the victory ; but it was an action in which the Indians became tired, and deserted in great numbers, so that it was in reality of great importance to the Americans.

General Burgoyne moved on towards Saratoga, and General Gates followed him. Burgoyne, as if disposed to destroy the country which he could not conquer, set fire to all the dwelling houses in his way, and reduced them to ashes,—broke down all the bridges, and endeavoured to stop up the road, to delay his pursuers ; but the Americans were not long in surmounting such difficulties.

General Gates, anticipating the course that Burgoyne would take, placed his own troops in such situations as entirely surrounded the army of the enemy.

To deprive Burgoyne of his only hope of escape up the Hudson, General Gates ordered troops to guard all the fords, and defend them until his army should join them. General Burgoyne used every means to effect an escape, but his conquering course was run. Seeing his situation to be desperate, he made proposals for a surrender, and articles of capitulation were agreed to, by which the British soldiers were to march out of their camp, lay down their arms, and not to serve again in the war. They were to go to Boston, and thence

to England. This important victory was gained on the 16th October, and filled the people
with a strong confidence that they had the favour of God, and might take to themselves the
promise, " In war he shall redeem thee from
the power of the sword."

The event gave a new face to things in Europe, and the contest of the colonies began to
excite feelings of deep interest among the rival
nations of the continent. It was of the highest importance to the states to gain the aid of
those nations while they were so weak, and
without funds to carry on the war, and the
prospects of success were now so greatly increased, that those powers began to seek their
own advantage in forming friendly relations
with a country whose commerce was so great.

When the victory was known in Pennsylvania, some of the officers of the army were
so elated by it, that they were anxious immediately to make an attack on the enemy in Philadelphia, and the people generally approved
of the rash plan. Many, who only looked on
while their countrymen were toiling, thought
that they knew better than Washington how
to conduct the war, and they were loud in
their talk on the subject.

Washington knew well the condition of
both armies. His steady mind was not daz-
zled by the idea of the praise he should gain
by success, and he persevered in resisting
public clamour, when he knew that by yield-

ing to it he should endanger the interests of
his country His unyielding virtue saved his
army for more important services. He was
always in the best state of preparation that he
could by constant exertion effect, for meeting
an attack ; but was resolved not to commence
one.

Intelligence was brought to him that the
enemy in the city were preparing to march
out of it, and that it was the design of General Howe, as he said, to drive him beyond
the mountains.

This information was given by a female,
named Lydia Darrah, who resided in Second
street below Spruce street, opposite to General Howe's head-quarters, in Philadelphia.
Two of the British officers chose a back
chamber in her house, as a secure place to
hold private conversations in ; and on the 2d
December they told her they would be there
at seven o'clock, and remain late, and desired
that she and all her family would go to bed
early. She thought something that would be
important to the Americans was to be talked
of, and she placed herself in a situation to
overhear what was said, and understood from
the conversation that all the British troops
were to march out in the evening of the 4th,
to surprise General Washington in his camp.
Supposing it to be in her power to save the
lives of hundreds of her countrymen, she was
determined to try to carry this intelligence to

General Washington. She told her family she would go to Frankford, to the mill, where she always got her flour; and she had no difficulty in getting permission from Geneneral Howe to pass the troops on the lines. Leaving her bag at the mill, she hastened towards the American camp, and met an American officer, named Craig, whom she knew. To him she told the secret, and made him promise not to betray her, as her life might in that case be taken by the British. Craig hastened to General Washington with the information, and Lydia returned home with her flour.

General Howe marched on the 4th December, but found Washington expecting him; and, disappointed, he encamped within three miles of the Americans. An action was then expected by Washington, and he prepared for it.

One day passed in which small detachments from each army attacked each other, and then all remained again at rest. Another day was spent in the same manner, and Washington employed himself in giving directions to every division of his army, and in encouraging them to resist with calm bravery. General Howe suddenly broke up his camp, and marched his troops back to the city. His doing so was a proof that he doubted too much the result of a contest, when the Americans were in a favour able situation for meeting him.

CHAPTER V.

1777—1780.

As the severe cold increased, the sufferings of the troops caused Washington great anxiety ; and he determined on seeking some better shelter for them than that of tents. He could not separate them with safety, and he determined on removing to a place called the Valley Forge, on the west side of the Schuylkill, about twenty-four miles distant from Philadelphia. The march of the army might have been traced by the marks of many naked, bleeding feet, on the frozen earth. The half perished men erected log huts, to shelter them from the piercing blasts, but their clothing was light; and when they lay down to rest, they had not blankets to cover them on their bare earthy beds. The difficulty of getting provisions was so great that they were often many days without bread, or any other kind of food, than that of a scanty portion of potatoes, and nuts, which they could gather from under the dried leaves in the woods. The regular order of an encampment was kept up, and there was no change except that of huts for tents.

In the year 1827, on that spot were collected several thousands of the inhabitants of this now free and prosperous land, to celebrate with "the voice of mirth and gladness," the ingathering of a rich harvest, given to them by that bounteous God who "clothes their pastures with flocks, covers over their valleys with corn, and crowns the year with his goodness."' This festival is yearly held.

What a contrast was the scene of that harvest-home, to that of the hut encampment! Should an American think of it, and not acknowledge with gratitude that it must have been the mighty hand of the great Ruler of the universe, that led those patriots through a wilderness of sufferings to the purchase of a land of freedom and prosperity for their children? and acknowledging this, can any one refuse to praise him for his goodness, and " offer unto him the sacrifice of thanksgiving?"

Washington heard that he was blamed for seeking even the hut shelter for his suffering troops, and he said, " It is much easier to censure by a good fireside, in a comfortable room, than to occupy a cold, bleak hill, and sleep under frost and snow, without either clothes or blankets."

Restless busybodies raised a report that he was wearied of his situation, and intended to resign it; in a letter to a friend, he said, " I can assure you, that no person ever heard me drop an expression that had a tendency to resignation. I have said, and I do still say, that there is not an officer in the United States that would return to the sweets of domestic life with more heart-felt joy than I should. But I would have this declaration accompanied by these sentiments, that while the public are satisfied with my endeavours, I mean not to shrink from the cause; but the moment her voice, not that of faction, calls upon me to resign, I shall do so with as much pleasure as ever wearied traveller retired to rest."

The faithful wife of Washington had no family to need her care at home, and when he was absent and deprived of its comforts, that home was cheerless to her. When it was possible, she was with him to share his hardships, and endeavour to contribute to cheer his sad prospects, by her attentions and expressions of calm, firm confidence, that better days would soon come. At the hut camp his table was furnished with no better food than could be procured for his troops; and his wife then shared his hard bread and few potatoes. Her willingness to do so, and her cheerful conduct, assisted to enliven the desponding, and encourage those who were cast down. Through the trying scenes of the long contest, the American women proved that they possessed patriotic feelings, by doing all in their power to aid their fathers, sons, brothers, and husbands, in the defence of their country.

They actively endeavoured to supply them with clothing, and to free them from anxiety

When it was possible, she was willing to share his hardships for the safety of themselves and their children, whom they were obliged to leave unprotected An extract from a letter, written in the gloomy December of 1776, will be a specimen of the sentiments expressed generally by American wives. " The country here is all in confusion ; the militia are to march in the morning. I will send a letter, but know not where it will find you. May God grant you health, and preserve you through this fatiguing campaign. I feel little for myself, when I think of the dangers to which you and so many of my brave countrymen are exposed. But I will not repine—God is all sufficient. I would not have you here, when your country calls, if one wish could bring you. Feel no care for me and our children ; through the mercy of our God, I have been enabled to conquer my fears, and do hope in his providence to meet you again in a better day. I think a decisive stroke must soon be given ; God grant that it may be in our favour."

Often obliged to conceal themselves and their children, in barns and wood-thickets, from the parties of English soldiers which overran the country, many were the fervent prayers which the American women breathed from those hiding places to the ever present God, whom they trusted would protect them. In his own good time, he fulfilled to them his promise, " My people shall dwell in a peaceable habitation."

While his army were in their log huts, Washington was not idle. He directed various means to be tried for obtaining supplies of provisions; and employed his mind in reflecting on the best plans to be pursued by the different commanders of the army. He prepared accounts for each state, of the number of troops which remained of those sent by it, and urged earnestly that more should be engaged. Congress was assembled in Lancaster, and appointed a committee to visit the camp, and Washington wrote a statement for them of all his plans for relieving the army.

While he was thus engaged, he received a letter from the English governor of New York, enclosing a resolution of Parliament to propose a reconciliation to the Americans; offers of pardon were made, but none to acknowledge their independence.

The governor requested General Washington to make this resolution known to his army. He sent the letter and paper to Congress, and expressed his surprise at the " extraordinary request of the governor." Congress immediately resolved to refuse accepting any offers from the English government, unless the independence of their country was acknowledged. General Washington enclosed this resolution to the governor, and requested him to make it known to the English army.

To show the settled determination of Congress on his point, and the spirit of devotion in which they had acted, it may be mentioned that Mr. Laurens, the President of Congress stated, in reply to a letter to him on the sub- ject, that it would be unnatural to suppose their minds less firm than " when destitute of all foreign aid, and even without expecta- tion of an alliance, when upon a day of gene- ral fasting and humiliation, in their houses of worship, and in the presence of God, they re- solved to hold no treaty with Great Britain unless they shall acknowledge the indepen- dence of these states." Men, who, in the ex- ercise of confidence in God's providence, and in humble prayer to Him, calmly resolve on any course, are not the persons to be diverted from their purpose by fear or the hope of gain. Such were the men to whom we owe our liberties, under the blessing of the God whom they worshipped.

Several letters were addressed to some members of Congress, by commissioners au- thorized by the British government, assuring them of honours and reward, if they would procure a reconciliation on the terms they of- fered—that is, to remain colonies. A propo- sal was made to Joseph Reed, a member from Pennsylvania, that he should have the best office in America under the king, and ten thousand pounds, if he could bring Con- gress to consent to the offers of the British. He replied that he was " not worth buying ; but, such as he was, the king of England was not rich enough to do it." The commissioners persisted for some time in their endeavours to succeed, and sent addresses to persons of every description in each state, with offers of pardon if they would return to their duty to the king, and threatenings of severe vengeance, if they did not: but their promises and threats were alike disregarded.

About this time Congress received intelligence from Silas Deane, Dr. Franklin, and Arthur Lee, their agents in France, that they had succeeded in making a treaty with the French nation. The joy throughout the country, when this was known, is inexpressible. That God, to whom their ardent prayers were offered in the time of distress, was not forgotten in the day of rejoicing. By order of Washington, the several brigades assembled, and their chaplains offered up public thanks to Almighty God for his mercies, and suitable discourses were delivered on the occasion.

The sufferings of the wounded soldiers at Valley Forge pained the heart of their commander, and he wrote: " I sincerely feel for the unhappy condition of our poor fellows in the hospitals, and wish my powers to relieve them were equal to my inclinations. Our difficulties and distresses are certainly great, and such as wound the feelings of humanity."

While he was thus humanely and actively employed in various ceaseless duties, slanderers were busy in secret, preparing new

anxieties for his mind. Unsigned letters were
sent to several members of Congress, containing base charges against him, and urging them
to endeavour to take from him the command
of their armies.

He received a letter from Patrick Henry,
governor of Virginia, enclosing one that had
been sent to him on the subject. Governor
Henry said, " While you face the armed
enemies of our liberty, and by the favour of
God have been kept unhurt, I trust our country will never harbour in her bosom the mis-
creant who would ruin our best supporter. I
cannot help assuring you of the high sense of
gratitude which all ranks of men in this, your
native country, bear you. I do not like to
make a parade of these things, for I know you
are not fond of it ; but the occasion will plead
my excuse."

After thanking him, Washington, in reply,
said, " All I can say is, America has, and I
trust ever will have, my honest exertions to
promote her interest. I cannot hope that my
services have been the best ; but my heart
tells me they were the best that I could render." He requested that the papers might all
be laid before Congress, as they contained, he
said, serious charges.

Pained, no doubt, by these cruel slanders,
yet his noble mind did not suffer them to influence his conduct towards those whom he
had cause to suppose were the authors of

them.   He said, " My enemies take an unge-
nerous advantage of me. They know I cannot
combat their insinuations, however injurious,
without disclosing secrets it is of the utmost
importance to conceal."

The only effect these attacks had, was to
excite the resentment of the people of the
United States against those who made them ,
and to bind still closer to their revered commander, the army from whom his secret enemies wished to remove him.   There was
something in his character which attached his
officers and troops to him so firmly, that no
distress nor sufferings could lessen the veneration they felt for him ; and he always acknowledged with praise their faithfulness and
attachment.

In describing their condition in the hut-
camp, he said, " For some days there has
been little less than a famine in the camp ; but,
naked and starving as they are, I cannot
enough admire the incomparable fidelity of the
soldiers, that they have not before this time
been excited to a general mutiny or disper-
sion."

The inhabitants of the surrounding country,
knowing this sad state of the army, were very
uneasy; one of them left his home, one day,
and as he was passing thoughtfully the edge
of a wood near the hut-camp, he heard low
sounds of a voice.   He stopped to listen, and
looking between the trunks of the large trees

he saw Gen. Washington engaged in prayer
He passed quietly on, that he might not disturb him ; and, on returning home, told his
family he knew the Americans would succeed, for their leader did not trust in his own
strength, but sought aid from the hearer of
prayer, who promised in his word, " Call
upon me in the day of trouble ; I will deliver
thee, and thou shalt glorify me." A female,
who lived at the Valley Forge when the army
was encamped there, told a friend who visited
her soon after they left it, that she had discovered that it was the habit of Washington to
retire to a short distance from the camp to
worship God in prayer. Many, who in " the
day of prosperity" have forgotten or neglected
to worship their Creator, will earnestly call
upon him in " the day of trouble," when they
feel that His power only can deliver them ;
but it was not thus with Washington ; it was
his constant custom as one of his nephews
has thus related : " One morning, at day-
break, an officer came to the general's quarters with despatches. As such communications usually passed through my hands, I took
the papers from the messenger and directed
my steps towards the general's room. Walk
ing along the passage which led to his door, I
heard a voice within. I paused, and distinctly recognised the voice of the general. Lis-
tening for a moment, when all was silent
around, I found that he was earnestly engaged

in prayer. *I knew this to be his habit*, and therefore retired, with the papers in my hand, till such time as I supposed he had finished the exercise, when I returned, knocked at his door, and was admitted." Thus, in obedience to Him whom he called " the Divine Author of our blessed religion," Washington, in the retirement of his chamber, prayed to his " Father who seeth in secret;" and truly his " Father, who seeth in secret," did "reward him openly."

Although the sufferings of the Americans, while encamped at the Valley Forge, were severe, yet, in after days, when those who had been engaged in the trying warfare, were enjoying the blessings of that independence for which they had toiled, they then could be sensible that they had been tried by their Creator to " humble them and prove them," that he might " do them good at the latter end."

When the gloomy winter was passed, Washington prepared, as far as he had the power, for the summer campaign ; but all the plans he formed for increasing his army were in a great degree disappointed. The favour of Divine Providence had been given in restraining their enemies from attacking them in their hut-encampment; want of provisions would have forced them out of it, and their sad condition as to clothing would have disabled them from remaining in the field unshel-

tered.   In February there were more than
three thousand men unfit for duty, from a want
of clothes ; and there were not more than five
thousand who could have attempted to resist a
well clad, well fed, and high spirited army.
The wisdom of their foes was " turned into
foolishness," or the feeble Americans would
have fallen beneath their power.

In the spring, to restrain as much as possible the parties which went from the city to
get provisions, and to form a guard for the security of the army at the Valley Forge, General Lafayette, with two thousand men, was
stationed at Barren Hill, about eight or ten
miles in front of the army.   When the English commander was informed of this, he sent
General Grant, with five thousand men, to
march quietly in the night, and place themselves between Lafayette and the hut-camp.
A detachment of militia, who were to have
guarded the roads in that direction, changed
their place without the knowledge of Lafayette; and at sunrise, 20th May, 1778, he
discovered that this large force of the enemy
was approaching in a way that would prevent
his retreat to the camp.

He immediately advanced at the head of the
column, as if to meet the enemy, while he directed the rest of his troops to move off rapidly
towards the Schuylkill, and, as he advanced,
he also approached the river.   General Grant
halted to prepare for battle ; and Lafayette di-

rected some of his troops to arrest the attention of those who had been placed to guard the ford, and he then passed so quickly over the river, with all his men, that he had possession of the high grounds by the time that his enemy could arive at the ford ; and they returned to the city without having accomplished the purpose for which they had been sent out.

When the English government knew of the treaty between France and America, they expected that a French fleet would be sent out, and in that case Philadelphia would be a dangerous situation for their army. Sir Henry Clinton took the place of Sir William Howe, and he was directed to remove the troops from the city. When General Washington heard of this, he formed his plan for acting. He wished to prevent the enemy passing through New Jersey with ease; and he directed the militia there to break down the bridges, and obstruct the roads as much as possible ; and he kept his own troops in readiness to move, so soon as the enemy should leave the city.

On the 18th June, 1778, they crossed at Gloucester Point, into New Jersey, and passed slowly on through Haddonfield towards Allentown. The numerous troops, with their baggage, formed a line of several miles in length.

General Washington put his troops into motion on the same day, and marched through Pennsylvania to Coryell's Ferry, where the town of New Hope has since been built ;

there he crossed the Delaware, and advanced towards Kingston in New Jersey. The English army had marched to Monmouth; and Washington, having determined on attacking them gave orders to the officers of his army, and marched towards Monmouth, where he met the enemies of his country on the 28th June The heat of the air was powerful; but more powerful still were the uncontrolled passions of human nature; and the dreadful work of battle commenced, and continued until the beams of the glowing sun were all withdrawn, and the dark, cool shade of night fell upon the awful scene, and stopped the fearful work.

The American army rested on their arms; and General Washington threw himself at the foot of a tree, to gain a little ease after the fatigues of the anxious day. He expected that the light of dawn would be the signal for renewing the action; but the English moved silently away in the night, and the morning showed the mournful scenes of a battle ground —man deprived of life and all its hopes by his fellow man; or wounded, to linger in uncomforted sufferings. Every real Christian will rejoice, that there is a divine promise that the time shall come, when he who is " the Mighty God," will exercise his power as " the Prince of Peace," and bring all hearts into subjection to the mild precepts of the gospel, so that " nation shall not lift up sword against nation, neither shall they learn war any more."

The victory was claimed by both armies. General Washington knew that the English could gain a favourable situation before he could overtake them, and he determined or not attempting it; but moved towards the north river, while the enemy passed on, and crossed over to New York.

Before General Washington reached the place he intended to encamp on, he received a letter from Congress, informing him that a French fleet had arrived off the coast of Virginia, and that Congress wished him immediately to form some plan, in the execution of which the fleet could assist him. The admiral of the fleet proposed attacking the English at Newport, in Rhode Island. General Washington consented to this, and made preparations for doing so. American troops, commanded by General Sullivan, were soon in readiness to besiege the town, but waited for some days for the French fleet to appear and assist them. Feeling confident that it was near, Sullivan commenced the siege. The fleet in a few days was in sight, but then was moved off to meet the English fleet which had sailed from New York. They were preparing for an action, when a violent storm separated them, and injured several of their ships. The English fleet then sailed back to New York, and the French admiral D'Estaing informed General Sullivan, that he could not return to Newport, but would sail to Boston to repair his ships.

Sullivan was sadly disappointed by this re-solution, as it would oblige him to give up the siege, in which he had every prospect of success, if assisted by the fleet. General Lafay-ette went to the admiral to endeavour to pre-vail on him to remain, but his efforts were vain. General Sullivan then, in giving his or-ders to his troops, said they must " endea-vour to do for themselves, what their French friends had refused to aid them in ;" but he found it would be useless to continue the siege, and he withdrew from Newport. He was followed by the English, and had a short but severe battle on the 29th August, and then crossed over to the main land. The next day a large force and several English ships arrived at Newport, so that if he had remained one day longer, his army must have been destroyed or taken. The French admiral was very much offended by what General Sullivan had said; and the people in Boston were so much displeased with the conduct of the admiral, that it was feared he would not be able to get assistance there to repair his ships.

With care like that of an anxious parent for a child, Washington watched every occurrence that would be likely to injure the interests of his country : and this event gave him great uneasiness. He endeavoured to calm the of-

fended parties ; and in this work of peace-
making he was aided by the amiable Lafay
ette, who was as deservedly dear to his own
countrymen, as he was to the Americans. A
few letters passed between Washington and
the admiral, and at last good humour was restored.

When the English fleet was repaired, it
sailed to Boston, to blockade the French ; but
a storm again carried it out to sea, and in the
beginning of November the French fleet left
Boston and sailed for the West Indies.

As it seemed probable that there would be
a war in Europe, in which France would take
a part, General Lafayette wished to offer his
services to his own country. General Washington expressed a wish to Congress that Lafayette, instead of resigning his commission,
might have leave of absence for any time that
he wished; Congress complied with this, and
Lafayette returned to France. A part of the
English army was sent in the fleet of Commo-
dore Hyde Parker, to the southern states ; and
as there was no prospect of doing any thing in
the northern or middle states in a winter campaign, Washington placed his army in huts,
the main body in Connecticut, and portions
on both sides of the Hudson river, and about
West Point, and at Middle Brook.

In preparing for the next campaign, Congress were less active than the anxious mind
of Washington thought absolutely necessary,

for they expected that the alliance formed with
France would be of great importance to aid
them in soon ending the war.   Washington
used every effort to prevent this false security
injuring the cause he was so desirous to promote; and his wisdom and sound judgment
could discover the fatal consequences of becoming less active in preparations for defence.
The English troops which had been sent to
Georgia, commanded by General Provost and
Colonel Campbell, had succeeded in taking
entire possession of that state ; and thus victorious there, it was probable they would attempt
to do the same in the other southern states.
In writing on the subject of increasing every
effort to raise more troops, Washington said—
" I have seen without despondency even for a
moment, the hours which America called her
gloomy ones ; but I have beheld no day since
the commencement of hostilities, when I have
thought her liberties in such imminent danger as at present."   But it was also about
this time, that reviewing the history of the
year in a letter to a friend, he observed :—
' *The hand of Providence is so conspicuous
in all this, that he must be worse than an in-
fidel that lacks faith, and more than wicked,
that has not gratitude to acknowledge his
obligations.*"

An occurrence in his army caused in his
mind a new care. The Indians on the frontiers
of the states had been practising their barba-

rous warfare, in connexion with some of the equally barbarous white settlers.

Washington determined on sending troops there for the relief of the suffering inhabitants; and gave orders for this purpose to the officers whom he intended should command these troops   The officers of one of the regiments entered into an agreement not to march, until Congress had paid them all that was due to them; and to resign, if it was not done in three days.

When their commander was informed of this he was much distressed. He knew the sufferings which had driven them to this determination; but he dreaded the ill consequences of it, and immediately wrote to the officers as their friend, as well as their commander.

He said, " The patience and perseverance of the army have been, under every disadvantage, such as to do them the highest honour, both at home and abroad; and have inspired me with an unlimited confidence in their virtue, which has consoled me amidst every perplexity and reverse of fortune, to which our affairs, in a struggle of this nature, were necessarily exposed.   Now that we have made so great a progress to the attainment of the end we have in view, so that we cannot fail, without a most shameful desertion of our own interests, any thing like a change of conduct would imply a very unhappy change of prin-

ciples, and a forgetfulness as well of what we
owe to ourselves as to our country. The service for which the regiment was intended does
not admit delay. I am sure I shall not be
mistaken in expecting a prompt and cheerful
obedience." The rest of the letter contained
assurances of his affectionate interest in their
concerns, and his constant endeavours to procure for them all the relief in his power.

The officers replied, that they sincerely regretted having given him uneasiness, but that
they had been driven to the course they had
pursued, by being without the means of sup-
plying their families with food. They assured
him they did not intend to disobey his orders
and that they had "the highest sense of his
abilities and virtues." They marched at the
time appointed, and their faithful commander
made such earnest representations to Congress,
on the subject of making provision for them,
that he was in a good degree successful in obtaining it.

Early in the spring, he received information
that the English in New York were making
preparations for some expedition ; and he suspected they would attempt to take possession
of the forts on the Hudson river. At the commencement of the Highlands, through which
the river winds, the Americans had erected a
fort, which they called Lafayette. It was on
the west side of the Hudson, and opposite to
it was a high piece of ground, called Stony

Point. They began to form defences there,
but before they were completed, a large force
from New York was sent out against the
workers, and they were obliged to retreat.
The English then fired upon Fort Lafayette
from Stony Point, while their ships prepared
to attack it from their situation higher up the
river. To prevent the entire destruction of
all the troops in it, the commander surrendered the fort, and the enemy then finished the
works on Stony Point, and placed troops there
for its defence. A part of their army then
marched into Connecticut; the militia of that
state assembled immediately, and made a
brave resistance, but it was feeble, compared
to the power of their foes. The governor of
New York, General Tryon, commanded them,
and he excused himself for burning the towns,
by saying it was " to resent the firing of the
rebels from their houses, and to mask a re-
reat."

It was in the summer of this year, that General Washington took measures to suppress
the habit of profane swearing which prevailed
in the army. The following general order is
sufficiently illustrative of his views of that
most vulgar and impious practice.

"HEAD QUARTERS, *Mores' House,*
"Thursday, July 29th, 1779.
"Many and pointed orders have been issued
against that unmeaning and abominable cus-

tom, SWEARING. Notwithstanding which, with much regret the general observes that it prevails, if possible, more than ever—his feelings are continually wounded by the oaths and imprecations of the soldiers; whenever he is in hearing of them, the name of that Being from whose bountiful goodness we are permitted to enjoy the comforts of life, is incessantly imprecated and profaned in a manner as wanton as it is shocking: for the sake therefore of religion, decency, and order, the general hopes and trusts, that officers of every rank would use their influence and authority to check a vice which is as unprofitable as it is wicked and shameful. If officers would make it an invariable rule to reprimand, and if that does not do, to punish soldiers for offences of this kind, it could not fail of having its intended effect."

On the first intelligence of the invasion of Connecticut, Washington sent troops to aid the militia of that state; but before they could be useful, the English troops were recalled to New York. This movement was occasioned by the activity of the Americans in the Highlands.

Washington had determined on endeavouring to recover Stony Point; he thought that success in this would draw the enemy from their destructive work of burning the towns on the coast. The troops chosen for this attempt were commanded by General Wayne. They marched fourteen miles over a rough, mountainous country, in the middle of July, and then had to pass a long marsh. They succeeded in approaching the fort in quietness in the middle of the night, and made an attack with their bayonets, with so much bravery, that they got possession of it without a single gun being fired by them.

As General Washington expected, this success caused the English general to recall his army from Connecticut, and he determined to employ all his force, by land and water, to retake the fort. Washington knew they would certainly succeed, he would not expose his troops to destruction, and he withdrew them from Stony Point and placed them at West Point, which he made the head-quarters of his army. Soon after he had done so, one of his officers, Major Lee, formed a plan for surprising the English troops that were stationed at Paules-Hook. He was successful in executing his plan, and took a large number of them prisoners.

The French fleet returned from the West Indies, and arrived off the coast of Georgia; and, assisted by the American troops, who were commanded by General Lincoln, made an unsuccessful attack upon the English, who had possession of Savannah. The fleet then left America again.

In the course of that season, the noise of war was heard in almost every portion of the land.   Gen. Sullivan was sent against the Indians on the frontiers.   English troops entered the newly settled parts of Massachusetts, and a large force was also busy in the south.

When the month of December was almost passed, General Washington placed his army in two hutted-camps.   One near West Point, for the security of the posts on the North river;   and the other near Morristown, New Jersey.

Winter quarters afforded but little rest to his anxious mind, for his troops were destitute of provisions,—so much so, that he wrote to Congress that at one time he thought it would be impossible to keep them together, for they had to eat " every kind of horse food but hay;" and yet, said he, " they bore it with heroic patience, and not one mutiny was excited."

A considerable force, commanded by Sir Henry Clinton, was sent from New York to the southern states, and was actively employed there during the winter.   An army and fleet attacked Charleston, which was bravely defended by General Lincoln and a few troops, but the power of their enemies could not be resisted long, and Gen. Lincoln was obliged to surrender to them.   His troops, and the citizens of Charleston who had given their aid to defend it, were considered as prisoners of

of troubles," he was not forsaken by God, and he might have used the language of trust, "Thou wilt revive me: thou shalt stretch forth thy hand against the wrath of our enemies, and thy right hand shall save us."

The difficulty of obtaining food, and the uncertainty of receiving even the small pay that was due to them, had greatly depressed the soldiers; and the patience of some was almost worn out. Two regiments declared their resolution to return home, and it was with some difficulty they were prevented, and induced to persevere in the performance of their duty. The paper money, which was the only kind Congress had to pay them with, was becoming every day less in value; and when they did receive it, four months' pay of a soldier would not purchase a bushel of wheat for his family; nor would the pay of an officer supply him with the shoes he needed.

The discontent which was arising in the army was known by the English commander in New York, and he secretly sent into their camp a paper, which contained artful persuasions to induce the discontented to give up the cause in which they had suffered so much. He thought, too, that the inhabitants of the surrounding country were wearied with endeavouring to supply an army with provisions; and he sent five thousand men, commanded by General Knyphausen, with the

expectation that they would not meet any opposition from the people ; and that some portion of the American soldiers would be willing
to join them.

They landed at night at Elizabethtown
Point, in New Jersey, and marched early the
next morning towards Springfield ; but they
soon were convinced that they were mistaken
as to the manner in which they would be
welcomed by the inhabitants and the army.
On the first appearance of the confident invaders, the militia of the state assembled, and
though their number was not sufficient to make
a stand against them at any one place, they did
not lose sight of them, but made irregular attacks whenever their situation would admit of
doing so.

A flourishing settlement, called the Connecticut Farms, was entirely reduced to ashes ;
and the wife of the clergyman, who was sitting in her house surrounded by her children,
was shot by a soldier who saw her through
the window. This savage act was condemned
by his commander, but it had the effect of
rousing all the people to resistance.

The same day on which the English marched from Elizabethtown, Washington marched
with his army to meet them near Springfield,
and there prepared for an engagement ; but
the enemy retreated in the night to the place
where they had landed. He then determined
to march for the protection of the forts in the

Highlands, for which he thought the British were aiming; but soon after he left Morristown, the enemy moved on to Springfield and burned it, in spite of the efforts of General Greene, whom Washington had left there with a thousand men. The troops of Greene took a station in the heights, from which they could annoy the army, and prevent their progress, and Sir Henry Clinton returned to Staten Island.

When General Lafayette returned to France, he was received with great favour; and that kind and faithful friend of Americans used all his influence to persuade the French government to send them assistance. He succeeded in his efforts; and when he had done so, as his own country did not need his services, he returned to America, to bring the tidings that a French fleet would soon sail for the United States.

Lafayette was received by his friend Washington with joy and affection. He had determined to remain, and share again his toils and dangers by resuming his situation in the army. He was welcomed by Congress with respect, and they immediately began to make more active preparations for the next campaign, in the hope that it would be the last one. They called upon the different states to raise more troops, and give more aid to provide for them. This call was attended to; but the expected aid was slowly given. A number of citizens of Philadelphia, consulted together to determine on the most effectual way in which they could give assistance. An extract from the resolution they formed, will show their plan : " We, the subscribers, deeply impressed with the sentiments that on such an occasion should govern us, in the prosecution of a war, on the event of which our own freedom, and that of our posterity, and the freedom and independence of the United States, are all involved, hereby severally pledge our property and credit for the several sums specified and mentioned after our names, in order to support the credit of a bank, to be established, for furnishing a supply of provisions for the armies of the United States." This was the first bank in the United States, and the amount of the subscription to it was three hundred thousand pounds. Several private contributions were sent to the suffering troops from individuals ; but all that was done was insufficient for the relief that was needed ; and so late as the last of June, General Washington wrote to Congress, to urge them to further efforts, and show them the great necessity for more aid.

The state of his army caused him distress and vexation. He felt for the officers, as he knew they must suffer mortification from the exposure of their condition to the well fed and well clothed French troops, who were expected soon to arrive. He said in his letter

on the subject to Congress—" For the troops
to be without clothing, at any time, is highly
injurious to the service and distressing to our
feelings; but the want will be more peculiarly
mortifying, when we come to act with those
of our allies. It is most sincerely to be wished that there could be some supplies of clothing furnished to the officers.   There are a
great many whose condition is still miserable.
It would be well for their own sakes, and for
the public good, if they could be furnished.
They will not be able, when our friends come
to co-operate with us, to go on a common rou-
tine of duty; and if they should, they must,
from their appearance, be held in low estimation."

This picture of the state of the American
army shows the strength of the patriotism
which influenced them.   They felt severely,
but no sufferings could induce them to give up
a cause in which they believed they were exercising virtuous principles.   Gaining a victory in battle might have caused them to be
loudly praised; but their patient perseverance
in the endurance of their various trials, is
much more worthy of remembrance and admiration, than the heroism displayed in a battle
would be.

The American females were not inactive in
that time of need; they employed themselves
in making up clothing for the destitute soldiers, and in many instances denied themselves

the use of comforts, that they might cast a
mite into this treasury.

Another cause for anxious care was given
to Washington, in the uncertainty of the number of troops he would probably have under
his command from the different states. It was
very important for him to know this, in forming his plans for acting with the French fleet.
In writing to Congress on the subject, he said
—" The interest of the states, the honour and
reputation of our councils, the justice and
gratitude due to our allies—all require that I
should, without delay, be enabled to ascertain
and inform them, what we can or cannot undertake. Delay may be fatal to our hopes."
In this vexing state of uncertainty, he did not
indulge the wayward feeling that he might be
less active in the performance of his duty, because others, who were as much concerned
in the advantage to be gained, were neglectful
of theirs. He engaged his mind in forming
various plans, with the hope of obtaining the
assistance needful for executing them. He
was anxious to attempt getting possession of
New York, which was the stronghold of the
enemies of his country ; and feeble as the
hope of success was, he cherished it.

In July he heard that the French fleet had
arrived at Rhode-Island ; and it was necessary that he should immediately determine
on some particular plan in which the fleet
could give assistance. His favourite one of

attacking New York, was resolved upon, and
he wrote to Congress his determination. General Lafayette carried to the French admiral the plan which Washington had formed.
A day in August was appointed on which it
was expected the fleet might sail for New
York ; and the American army was to assemble at Morrisiana, in readiness to be aided by
the fleet in the proposed attack.   Before the
appointed day arrived, a British fleet came
from England, which, in addition to that already at New York, made a force much
greater than that of the French fleet, which
they immediately determined to attack, as
it lay before Newport, at the same time that
Sir Henry Clinton should attack that town
with his troops.

When General Washington heard of this
plan, he sent information of it to the French
admiral; and resolved, that in the absence of
the troops who were to leave New York, he
would attempt to take possession. He added
to his army all the troops that could be
spared with prudence from West Point, and
was marching hastily to New York, when
Sir Henry Clinton suddenly returned ; he had
heard such accounts of the situation of the defences at Newport, that he had given up his
intention to attack it.   Washington and his
army were greatly disappointed, for he knew
it would be rash to attempt attacking the city
without the aid of a fleet, when it was so well

guarded by one ; but he did not give up the
hope of being assisted, and wrote to the French
admiral on the subject. Several letters passed
from one to the other, but they concluded that
they could undertand the plan better, if they
saw each other to converse on it ; they agreed
to do so, and General Washington went to
Hartford in Connecticut, to meet the admiral
on the twenty-first day of September.

While he was absent, the fierce but artful
passion of revenge was busy in the heart of an
American, forming a plot of treason. When
the English had left Philadelphia, General
Arnold was placed there to take the command,
as it was a situation in which he could have the
rest which seemed to be necessary for the recovery of the wounds which he had received
in Canada. His courage and military talent
caused him to be highly regarded as an officer, and his countrymen were desirous that
he might be able again to take an active part
in the war. His bodily strength was soon
restored; but the integrity of his mind was
feeble : and he who had endured hardships
with bravery, and had been a hero in battle,
was overcome by the indulgence of ease, and
became a coward in his resistance of temptations to the practice of vice. One of the
many paths which are on the " broad way
that leadeth to destruction," is called the *path
of pleasure.* Arnold, who had toiled through
dangers, and fought for liberty with bravery

and ardour, entered that delusive path, and
soon became the slave of its weakening influence.   Whilst his former companions in the
field of battle were persevering courageously
in the defence of their country, and suffering
from the want of food and clothing—he was
engaged in dissipation, and was wasting a fortune in the gratification of idle vanity.   He
became involved in debt; and then dishon-
estly used every means within his power, to
get possession of the property of others.   His
ill conduct was at length made known to Congress, and they appointed a court of officers
of the army, to examine the charges brought
against him.

His accusers had no difficulty in proving
what they asserted, and the court sentenced
him to receive a reproof from General Washington; which they considered a truly severe
punishment.   He received reproof from stern
virtue with feelings of bitter resentment.
Vice had so hardened his heart, that the consciousness of deserving punishment had not
the effect of softening it to repentance; and
to plan for revenge against the officers who
had sentenced him, and the upright and noble
man who had reproved him, became the employment of his thoughts.

His depraved mind could readily practise
deception; and he said he was desirous to be
again placed in a situation to be useful to his
country.   He expressed a desire so frequently,

and with such seeming sincerity, that General Washington offered to him the command of a division of the army, when he was preparing to attack New York, in the absence of Sir Henry Clinton. Arnold said that his wounds had rendered him too feeble, to engage in very active duties, and declined accepting this offer. General Washington could not feel any suspicions of his resentful intention; though he was surprised at his unwillingness to use an opportunity for recovering the favourable opinion of the public.

The state of New York was particularly interested in the safety of West Point; and some important inhabitants of that state, who had a high opinion of the military talents of Arnold, and believed him to be faithful in his attachment to his country, applied to General Washington to place him there; as he might be very useful without much bodily exertion. This was the very situation which Arnold was anxious to obtain; and after writing to General Washington on the subject, he went to the camp to see him, and urge the request. The General, trusting his professions, and believing that he would be very capable of performing the military duties of such a station, gave to him the command. Rejoicing that he had been thus far successful in his deceptive plan, Arnold informed Sir Henry Clinton, that he was anxious to return to his duty as an English subject, and repented having violated his

allegiance to his king. In true repentance
there is always a desire to benefit those against
whom the fault has been committed; and
Arnold wished to make his profession of repentance seem sincere, by offering to do all
in his power to place his country again in a
state of dependence.

When he went to West Point, he wrote to
Sir Henry, that he would manage the troops
stationed there, so that he might, on attacking
them, readily make them his prisoners, or
else entirely destroy them. The English
general must have despised and distrusted the
traitor, and he ought to have scorned the proposal of using such cowardly means for subduing the Americans; but to get possession
of West Point was so desirable, that he gladly
received the base offer, and said he would appoint an officer to correspond with Arnold on
the subject.

The officer chosen for this degrading duty
was Major André. He was young, and had
been expensively educated, and his disposition
was so frank and amiable, that he was es-
teemed by all who became acquainted with
him. As an officer he was brave and faithful,
and was a favourite in the army. His friends
were strongly and tenderly attached to him,
and felt a perfect confidence in the strength
of his virtuous principles. But the foundation
of those principles was a wrong one; they
were placed on what he considered to be the

duty he owed to men, and not on that which he owed to God. When Sir Henry Clinton informed him of the employment he intended to give him, he consented to take a part in deception and treachery, and by doing so, lost his claim to integrity.

Several letters passed between Arnold and André, signed by the feigned names of Gustavus and Anderson ; but the plan of treason could not be safely understood without some conversation on the subject, and Arnold sent a pass, or written permission for André to go in the character of a person on business, past the guards at West Point, to a house near the out-post, where he promised to meet him : in the pass, he was called John Anderson. An English sloop of war, named the Vulture, was sent up the Hudson to take André as near to West Point as possible, without the risk of exciting suspicion. He was rowed in a small boat to the shore, and arrived in safety at the place appointed by Arnold. Night was chosen to veil from human eyes the plottings of treachery ; but " an All-seeing eye," to which " the darkness is as the noon day," rested on the deluded and erring André. And a power, from which no human strength or wisdom can deliver, was preparing a dreadful punishment for his wanderings from the path of virtue.

The night was spent in deeply interesting conversation, and the morning dawned before

all the parts of the dark plot were well under
stood.   André could not return to the vessel
by the light of day, with any hope of safety ,
and Arnold assured him that he could conceal
him until night, and for this purpose took
him within the posts, and remained with him
all day.   The Vulture had been noticed from
the fort, and fired on, and the commander
thought it necessary to move to a greater distance down the river.   When daylight had
again faded from the sky, and the hour of darkness had come, for which no doubt André
had anxiously watched, he left his place of
concealment, and expected to be quickly conveyed to the vessel from which he had come
the night before ; but it was removed to so
great a distance, that he could not prevail on
any boatman to take him to it, and Arnold
did not dare to aid him in persuading them.

Sadly perplexed, André was obliged at
length to determine on passing to New York
by land.   This was a perilous attempt ; for
parties of militia were employed in watching
all the roads leading from the Highlands to
that city. Arnold insisted on his changing his
dress for a plain one, and wrote a pass for
him, desiring the guards and militia to " permit John Anderson to go to the White Plains,
on business of great importance."

With this permit he passed all the out
guards with safety ; and was riding on with
a feeling of security, when near to Tarrytown,

a young man sprung from a thicket by the
road side, and seized the bridle of his horse
In the first practice of deception an ingenuous
mind is timid ; and André, though brave when
acting truly, became a coward when he was
conscious that he was a deceiver. He forgot
his pass in the moment of need, and in a hur-
ried tone of alarm, asked the man where he
was from ? " From below," was the reply ;
and supposing this meant from New York,
André said hastily, " So am I ;" and added,
that he was a British officer, who was going on
important business, and begged that he might
not be detained a moment. Two more young
men then came from the woods ; and he discovered too late that they all were Americans : their names were David Williams, John
Paulding, and Isaac Vanwert. He offered to
give them his valuable watch, a purse of gold,
and the promise of a large reward from the
English commander, if they would allow him
to pass.

All his offers were disregarded, and he was
obliged to submit to be searched. The papers he had received from Arnold were in his
boots ; his captors took possession of them,
and conducted him to a militia officer named
Jameson. André, anxious for the safety of
Arnold, asserted to Jameson that his name
was John Anderson, and requested him to
send immediately to West Point, and inform
General Arnold that he was there. Jameson

could not believe that Arnold was connected
with André in a plot of treachery, and he immediately complied with his request. When
André thought that Arnold had time to escape,
he again acknowledged his real character;
and Jameson sent an express to Gen. Washington, with the papers that had been found
in André's boots; and André wrote to him an
account of the manner in which he had been
captured, and the reason of his being disguised.

General Washington was returning from
Hartford, and the express took a road different from that on which he was travelling, and
thus missed him. He had sent to inform Arnold that he would be at West Point to breakfast; but stopping to examine some of the important passes in the mountains, he was detained later than he expected. Several officers,
in expectation of seeing their loved commander, were breakfasting with Arnold, when
he received a letter from Jameson informing
him of the capture of John Anderson. With
an appearance of calmness, he rose and left
the room; but his wife saw a change in his
countenance and followed him. With a few
hasty words, he told her of his danger, and
left her, to return to the breakfast room. He
made an excuse for leaving the officers so
hastily, by telling them that he had forgotten
to give some orders which were needful for
receiving the commander-in-chief with the re-

spect due to him, and that he must immediately attend to this duty.

He was quickly down on the shore, and ordered a sergeant and six men to enter a boat, and row him immediately to the sloop Vulture, which still was at anchor below the fort. The sergeant did not hesitate one moment, for he thought that General Arnold was going with a flag of truce, on business of importance to the American cause, and he soon placed him on board of the vessel. When Arnold felt himself safe, he told the sergeant that he did not intend to return, as he had determined to enter the service of the king of England, and he endeavored to persuade him to do the same. The sergeant and his men answered, that "If General Arnold liked the king of England, he might serve him; but they loved their country better, and intended to live and die in the support of its independence." Arnold then proposed to the commander of the Vulture to detain the men as prisoners; but he would not consent to so disgraceful an act.

By the time that General Washington arrived at West Point, the plan of treachery was known; but it was too late to secure the traitor. He requested to see Mrs. Arnold, and found her in a state of extreme distress. She begged him not to injure her, and was so violent in her feelings that he found it was vain to attempt to calm her by assuring her that she should be treated with kindness and respect. He left her in the care of her female servant, and sent for an officer whom he knew was strongly attached to Arnold, and who commanded one of the most important posts in the Highlands. When the officer came, Washington said to him, "Colonel, we have been deceived, Arnold is a traitor ; your post may be attacked to-night ; go back to it without delay, and defend it bravely, as I know you will." This generous confidence excited the feelings of the officer so much, that for some moments he was unable to reply ; but when he could speak, he said, "Your excellency has more than rewarded all that I have done, or ever could do for my country."

Arnold wrote to General Washington by the return of the boat which had conveyed him to the vessel. The daring insolence of his letter raised a glow on the cheek of Washington, but the first words he spoke after reading it, were dictated by the benevolent feelings of his heart. He desired that Mrs. Arnold might be relieved from her fears for the safety of her husband, by being told that he was secure from pursuit. Preparations were made for the defence of West Point, in case the enemy should attack it ; but Sir Henry Clinton would not venture to make the attempt, when he could not be aided by the treason of its commander.

When the fate of André was to be determined the general officers of the army met to examine him, and inquire into all the circumstances attending the dark plot in which he had been engaged, that they might judge whether he must be considered as a spy. He was treated with great tenderness, and was told that he might refuse to reply to any questions that would lead to his condemnation; but his mind, which had no doubt been engaged in solemn reflection, could no longer willingly practise deception, and he acknowledged the part he had been acting, so that it was not necessary to examine one witness.

With the hope of forming some excuse for him, it was said that he had gone to West Point with a flag of truce. He was asked if this was true; he replied, " Had I come with a flag, I might have returned with a flag." An American officer, who had a hope that he might yet be saved from condemnation, began to say to him that perhaps he might be exchanged for Arnold,—" Stop," said André, " such a proposal can never come from me." All the circumstances which he confessed, led the officers to determine that he deserved the character of a spy, and death is the sentence which the stern laws of war pass upon such a character.

Universal sorrow was felt for the sad and disgraceful close of life to which this young officer was brought by his departure from the path of rectitude. General Washington, in a private letter, expressed his estimation of the character of André; and perhaps never performed with so much reluctance any painful duty, as he did that of signing his sentence of death. This sentence was executed soon after, when André was hung, according to the usage of war in such cases. Arnold wrote several letters on the subject to General Washington, but he did not notice them; and directed that his baggage should all be sent to him, and that Mrs. Arnold should be carefully conducted to New York, where he was.

We are so ready to forget how unbounded and wonderful the power of God is, that we think and speak of events, which we consider trifling, as if they were not directed by him; but to say that any event happens " by chance," or " by accident," has no meaning, unless chance and accident are used as names for the secret workings of Divine power, which overrules the smallest occurrence as certainly as the greatest event. In every circumstance connected with Arnold's plot of treason, might be traced that Providence which can make the smallest accident defeat the wisest plans of man; and prove that " A man's heart deviseth his way, but the Lord directeth his steps."

The disappointed baseness of Arnold was made, by Him who ruleth all things, to be useful to his country. Arnold sent addresses to the officers and soldiers of the American army, to persuade them to follow his example, assuring them that if they did so, they would be liberally rewarded. These addresses had the effect of uniting the Americans more firmly than ever; and the indignation which they felt, animated them to more exertions to prove that they were determined to persevere in the defence of their country, and despised the man who had forsaken the cause of freedom.

Arnold was the only American officer who, through all the course of the war, deserved the name of traitor; and he most truly merited it; for, after he had joined himself to the enemies of his country, he was active in his endeavours to plan and perform deeds that would be most likely to injure it, and cause distress to his countrymen; but those endeavours were made to produce good for those against whom they were directed.

The account which he gave to Sir Henry Clinton of the weak and suffering state of the American army, caused him to feel a security and confidence in his own strength, which in several instances was advantageous to them. It has been said, that when all " the probable consequences of his plot, had it been successful, came to be considered, and the *seeming* accidents by which it was discovered and defeated, all were filled with a kind of awful astonishment, and the devout perceived in the transaction the hand of Providence guiding America to independence."

CHAPTER VII.

1780—1781.

In his conversation with the French admiral at Hartford, General Washington had been
convinced that he must give up his favourite
plan of attacking New York that season. The
admiral told him that he expected an addition
to his fleet; but that until it arrived, he had
not a force which he considered sufficient to
meet the English fleet, with any probability of
success, in an action. The two armies continued merely watching each other, until the
time arrived for going into winter quarters;
and the Americans were then stationed near
Morristown, and on the borders of New York
and New Jersey. The troops belonging to the
New England states were placed at West
Point, and on both sides of the river Hudson.

The scenery of West Point and its neighbourhood is beautifully wild; and is rendered
very interesting, by Washington having win-
tered there in that gloomy period of the revolution. Nearly six hundred feet above the
Hudson river, are the ruins of Fort Putnam,
which commanded the river below and above,
and also a passage which opens in the mountain. The large stones of which the fort was
constructed, it is said, were carried up the
steep path by men. On some of the hills are

remains of huts which were used by the army.
From a bank flows a remarkably cold and clear
spring, which is deeply shaded by trees and
is called Washington's spring. The old inhabitants of the surrounding country, who remembered the time when their defenders were
encamped on it, delighted afterwards to lead
strangers to notice a spring, the refreshing
water of which was daily used by their revered
protector. The season was too severely cold
to admit of a winter campaign, with troops almost destitute of clothing; and while they were
in winter quarters, and the never-idle Washington was engaged in preparing for employing them as soon as possible, the sad work
of war was going on in the southern States.
General Cornwallis, who had been left there
with an army, had, on the 16th August, attacked the Americans at Camden, and almost
entirely defeated them. He then seemed to
consider South Carolina as a conquered state,
and all the efforts that were made to resist
him, he called "acts of rebellion," and gave
orders that all persons who were found opposing the authority of the king of England,
should have their property destroyed, and be
treated with the greatest severity.

Some of the Americans had joined the English army, and Cornwallis heard that there
were others in the back part of the state of
North Carolina, who were willing to do so;
and he sent Major Ferguson with troops, to

unite with them in resisting and attacking all who continued faithful to the cause of independence.

Colonel Clarke, an American, who had left his home, in Georgia, when the English took possession of that state, collected a small company and attacked Augusta ; the English troops there were soon aided by an additional force, and Colonel Clarke retreated to the mountains. Ferguson heard of this, and resolved to stop him and his brave little band ; but some hardy mountaineers, from the western parts of Virginia and North Carolina, assembled quickly, and were joined by some militia from South Carolina. They marched rapidly towards Ferguson, who was posted on King's Mountain, and they attacked him so bravely, that in a short time his troops were entirely defeated. Ferguson was killed : three hundred of his party killed or wounded, and eight hundred made prisoners. One thousand five hundred stand of arms were taken. The result of this attack was very important,—for the disaffected Americans who escaped did not return to Cornwallis, and this loss obliged him to retreat out of North Carolina, where he had expected to be very successful.

He marched his army to Camden, to wait for more troops from New York, which Sir Henry Clinton was to send to him. While his army were encamped, near Camden, he was

obliged to detach parties of it to endeavour
to defeat an American officer named Marion,
who had a few brave men under his command.
They sometimes concealed themselves in
swamps and wood thickets, from which they
rushed out when any opportunity occurred for
an attack on the enemies of their country; or
when they could defend the helpless families
from which those foes were forcing provisions.
An anecdote of Marion will serve to show his
truly patriotic motives for enduring with patient fortitude the dangers and sufferings to
which he was exposed, by persevering in his
resistance of Cornwallis.

An English officer was sent to him to make
some proposals for an exchange of prisoners;
he received the officer with civility, and after
they had settled the business on which he
came, Marion invited him to stay and take
dinner with him. At the name of dinner, the
officer felt surprised; for on looking round,
he saw no appearance of any provisions, nor
of any place for preparing food. A few sun-
burnt militiamen were sitting on some old
tree stumps, with their powderhorns lying
beside them, and Marion looked as if he had
suffered from hunger.

The officer said he would accept his invitation; feeling curious, no doubt, to know
where the dinner was to come from. "Well,
Tom," said Marion to one of his men, "come.
give us our dinner." Tom took a pine stick,

and with it drew out some sweet potatoes from a heap of ashes, under which they had been placed to be roasted. He cleaned them first by blowing the ashes from them with his breath, and then by wiping them with the sleeve of his homespun shirt; and piling them on a piece of bark, he placed them between the English officer and Marion, on the trunk of the fallen pine tree on which they sat. The officer took one of the potatoes, and while he was eating it, began to laugh heartily. Marion looked surprised.

" Excuse me," said the officer, " but I was thinking how drolly some of my brother officers would look, if their government was to provide them with such dinners. But, no doubt, in general, you fare better?" " Rather worse," replied Marion, " for often we have not enough potatoes to satisfy our hunger." " Then, no doubt, though you are stinted in provisions, you draw good pay," said the officer. " Not one cent," replied Marion. " Then I do not see," said the officer, " how you can stand it." " These things depend on feeling," said Marion, " and I am happy. I would rather fight to obtain the blessing of freedom for my country, and feed on roots, than desert the cause, and gain by doing so, all the luxuries that Solomon owned."

When the officer returned to his commander he was asked why he looked so serious.—" I have cause, sir, to look so," was his reply.

' Why," said his commander, in alarm, " has Washington defeated Sir Henry Clinton ?' " No, sir: but more than that. I have seen an American general and his men without pay, and almost without clothes, living upon roots, and drinking water, and all for *liberty*. What chance have we against such men ?"

Cornwallis employed a very active officer, Colonel Tarlton, to draw Marion and his few followers from their secure retreats ; but he did not succeed, and he took his revenge on the surrounding country by plundering the inhabitants. He was drawn from this work by hearing of the appearance of the American general, Sumpter, who, with a company of militia, was approaching in an opposite direction. Sumpter had been a very active officer, but Cornwallis thought that he was entirely vanquished, and was greatly surprised to hear of his being again at the head of a respectable force.

He immediately determined to attack him in his camp, on Broad river, and sent a detachment from his army, commanded by Major Wemyss, for that purpose, which arrived several hours before day, and made the attack with vigour ; but Sumpter quickly drew his men into order, and they defended themselves so bravely, that their enemies were soon forced to retreat, with the loss of their commander. Sumpter then changed his situation, and Cornwallis directed Tarlton to follow and attack him.

Sumpter was placed with his troops on a steep hill, near the Tiger river, when Tarlton rashly attacked them, and was soon obliged to retire, in haste and disorder, leaving nearly two hundred men killed or wounded on the field. The loss of the Americans was three killed and four wounded. General Sumpter was severely wounded, and as he knew that it was probable Cornwallis would send a very powerful force against him, he thought it most prudent to disperse his men, and wait until his wound was healed to call them together again. For such was the spirit which animated men who were struggling for freedom that no desertion was feared. They came forth for the defence of their houses and families, and were ready to return whenever their services were needed.

The regular southern army was at that time very small, and the state of it was well described by Washington, in a letter to a friend, when he appointed General Greene to take the command of it; he wrote, " You have your wish in the officer appointed to the southern command. I think I am giving you a general : but what can a general do without men, without arms, without clothing, without stores, without provisions ?"

In December General Greene joined the army at Charlotte, in South Carolina; the whole number of troops placed under his command, did not amount to many more than two thousand, a greater part of whom were militia. He separated them into two divisions. and gave the command of one to General Morgan, and directed him to move to the south side of the Catawba river, while he marched down to the Pedee river, to encamp on the east side of it.

Thus situated, the army of Cornwallis lay between them, and he determined to attack one of them, but wished to leave it uncertain, as long as possible, which he would march against. Additional troops had been sent from New York, and were on their march to Camden. Cornwallis put his army in motion, and directed its course towards North Carolina, ordering the new troops to join him at the Catawba river, and charging Tarlton to move rapidly with a large detachment against Morgan, to "push him to the utmost, and, at all events, drive him over Broad river;" expecting, that if he escaped Tarlton, he would be met and defeated by the main body of the army.

A sudden swelling of the streams, which the army had to pass, delayed it a much longer time than Cornwallis had calculated for; and also prevented the new troops from joining him at the place he had appointed. Tarlton was more active with his troops, and reached Morgan before Cornwallis had arrived at the situation in which he intended to stop him, if he was forced to retreat.

General Morgan heard of these movements of his enemies, and knowing that his situation was a very dangerous one, he crossed the Pacolet river, and placed his men at the fording place, to defend it; but he soon heard that his pursuers had crossed the river six miles higher up, and he then quickly retreated to a spot amongst the pines, called the Cowpens. Halting there, Morgan consulted the officers of his little army as to the course of conduct that ought to be determined on, and they resolved to remain there and wait for the attack of their foes. They placed their troops on a piece of rising ground, in an open wood, and waited with firmness for their pursuers, who very soon made their appearance, and advanced perfectly confident that they should be victorious. This was on the 17th January, 1781.

Morgan and his officers gave their orders with so much calm judgment, and the soldiers attended to them so obediently and courageously, that Tarlton and his confident troops were driven back, and forced to fly, closely followed by the Americans, who made prisoners of five hundred of the soldiers and twenty-nine of their officers. They got possession, also, of eight hundred muskets, thirty-five baggage wagons, and a hundred horses. The Americans had less than eighty in killed and wounded. In this battle was Lieutenant-Colonel Washington, who, when a captain, behaved so bravely at the battle of Trenton. In the haste of pursuit he was separated from his regiment. Three English officers, one of whom was Tarlton, seeing this, turned quickly and attacked him. One aimed a blow at him, which was turned aside by a sergeant, who rushed forward to his aid. At the same moment the second officer made a stroke at him, but a young lad, who was too small to hold a sword, wounded the officer with a pistol, and thus saved Colonel Washington, who was engaged defending himself against Tarlton, who, finding that he could not succeed in his attack, turned to fly, and discharged a pistol, which wounded the horse of Col. Washington, but did not injure him.

Tarlton, in this personal conflict, received from Washington a wound in the hand; and it has been related, that he said to an American lady of Charleston, some time afterwards, "You appear to think very highly of Col. Washington; and yet, I have been told, that he is so ignorant a fellow, that he can hardly *write* his own name." To this silly insinuation she replied, "It may be the case, but no man can testify better than yourself, Colonel, that he knows how to make his *mark*."

Tarlton retreated with speed from the Cow pens, and did not stop until he reached the army of Cornwallis, which was at a distance of about twenty-five miles.

This victory was a very important one to the American cause; for, if Morgan's army had been defeated, Cornwallis would probably have attacked General Greene's with all his force, and no doubt with success, as his troops were so numerous ; and then all the southern states would have been in his possession.

The day after the battle the troops which Cornwallis had directed to join him arrived, and early the next morning he put all his army in motion, determining to attack Morgan with a force that would certainly destroy him. General Morgan marched quickly towards the Catawba river, and had crossed it only two hours before the English army reached its banks. As night was near, Cornwallis resolved not to attempt crossing the river until the day should dawn ; but when the dawn came, that gracious hand, which was conducting the Americans to independence through scenes of trial, had placed a barrier between Cornwallis and his expected prey, which all his power and wisdom could not enable him to overcome. A rain fell during the night, which seemed to be too trifling to make any increase in the depth of the river, but it was rendered impassable, and continued to be so for two days.

This providential delay of his pursuers, gave Morgan time to place his prisoners in a state of security, with the arms and stores which he had taken, and to refresh his wearied troops.

General Greene, on hearing of the battle at the Cowpens, was anxious to unite the two divisions of his army, and he travelled hastily to join General Morgan and aid him by his counsel, leaving the other division of his army under the command of General Huger.

When the swell of the waters had abated so that Cornwallis could cross the Catawba, he did so, and continued a rapid pursuit of the Americans, who were marching towards the Yadkin river, which they crossed on the 2d February, partly on flats, and partly by fording it, and had only time to secure all the flats from being used by their pursuers, when they appeared on the opposite bank of the river. Again the waters were commanded to aid the Americans, and, before their foes could prepare boats or flats to cross the Yadkin, a heavy rain and driving wind rendered it dangerous to make the attempt.

The stream continued to rise, and Cornwallis was obliged to move nearer to its source, where it was less deep, before he could venture to cross it.

A celebrated historian of the American Revolution, says:—" This second hairbreadth escape was considered by the Americans as a farther evidence that their cause was favoured by Heaven. That they, in two successive instances, should effect their passage, while their pursuers, who were only a few miles in their rear, could not follow, impressed the religious people of that settlement with such sentiments of devotion as added fresh vigour to their exertions in behalf of American independence."*

This delay enabled General Greene to move on as far as Guilford Court-House, where he was joined by the division he had left under the command of Huger.

When Cornwallis found that he could not prevent the union of these divisions, he resolved to endeavour to get between them and Virginia, so as to force them to an action, before they could receive any aid from troops which he heard were preparing in that state to join their countrymen.

General Greene knew that an action with so powerful an enemy must be fatal to his army; and he used great exertions to move it quickly on towards the Dan river, with the hope of being able to enter Virginia, before Cornwallis could overtake him. After many difficulties were overcome, General Greene succeeded in getting his troops safe across the river. They had marched forty miles in twenty-four hours, and the last boat in which they were crossing the river had scarcely touched the northern bank, when the army of Cornwallis appeared on the opposite shore.

General Greene and his little army had retreated for more than two hundred miles, without the loss of any men. The season was winter, the weather cold and wet, and

* Ramsay

the roads either deep or icy, and the troops almost naked and barefooted, and often had no
other food than corn grated on their tin can-
teens, in which they punched holes for that
purpose. The army of Cornwallis had passed
over the same roads, but they were well
clothed, and provided with strengthening food,
and were only prevented overtaking the Americans by the swelling of the waters in their
way. They were so often thus stopped,
when the Americans had just passed over in
safety, that the particular providence of God
was clearly seen in these delays, and General
Greene and his feeble army had cause to
praise the mercy which directed these means
for their preservation from a powerful foe.

When the American army entered Virginia,
Cornwallis gave up the pursuit of it, and
marched slowly to Hillsborough, at that time
the capital of North Carolina. He there raised
the standard of the king of England, and invited all the inhabitants of the state to assist
him in restoring the old government.

General Greene was resolved to prevent
his having entire possession of that state;
and when he had received the addition to his
army of a few hundred men, he re-crossed the
Dan river, and moved slowly towards Hillsborough. All the country around had been
searched for provisions to supply the English
army, and Cornwallis at length found that he
must remove to another situation, as it was

impossible for him to obtain what was need
ful where he was.

When he removed, Greene advanced, but
took care not to place his army where he
must be forced into an action before he should
be joined by more troops that he expected
from Virginia. When they came, he determined to risk a battle, and for that purpose
marched towards Guilford to meet Cornwallis
A very severe battle was commenced on the
15th March, and continued for some time,
with expectations of victory on both sides;
but after a considerable loss of men, Cornwallis was able to claim it, and Greene moved
his troops to a distance of twelve miles, where
he prepared for another attack, which he expected would soon be made. But Cornwallis
did not attempt it; for, though he had gained
a victory, he had lost so many men, and was
so unable to obtain provisions for his army,
that he was forced to retreat towards Wilming-
ton, where he expected he should get supplies
of food. As he passed on, he proclaimed,
that he had gained a great victory, and ordered
that there should be a general illumination.

A Mrs. Heyward, (whose husband had
been sent as a rebel in a prison ship to St.
Augustine, after the English had taken possession of Charleston,) closed the windows
of her house, when she heard of the order of
Cornwallis. An English officer entered it,
and said, " How dare you disobey the order

which has been given ?   Why is your house
not illuminated ?"   She replied, "Is it possible for me to feel joy ?   Can I celebrate a
victory of your army, and my husband a prisoner?"   The officer said, " The last hopes
of rebellion are crushed by the defeat of
Greene, and you shall illuminate."   " Not a
single light," said Mrs. Heyward, " shall be
placed, with my consent, in any window of
my house."   "Then" replied the officer, " I
will return with a party, and before midnight
level it with the ground."   "You have the power," said she, "and seem disposed to use it, but
you cannot control my determination, and I
will not illuminate." The officer left her and
did not return to execute his unfeeling threat.

Cornwallis moved his army into Virginia.
Some of the inhabitants of North Carolina
had deserted the cause of liberty, and placed
themselves under the protection of the English army.   To them of course, the removal
of that army from their state was a subject
of sorrow ; but to all those who had continued
firm in their determination to be independent
of the government of England, the deliverance
from the presence of those whose purpose was
to make them submit, occasioned great joy.
The name of Tarlton was heard with dread ;
for he was constantly practising some severity,
either in destroying the property of the faithful
Americans, or in punishing them whenever he
had an opportunity.   Some, in a moment of

terror, had professed a willingness to submit, but afterwards repented that they had done so, and determined on endeavouring to defend themselves; to such persons Tarlton showed no mercy. A young man who had acted in this manner, was afterwards taken prisoner, and Tarlton ordered him to be immediately hung by the road side; and placed on his back the declaration, "such shall be the fate of whoever presumes to cut him down." No one but the sister of the young man dared to disregard this threat; but she, with the resolution and tenderness of female attachment, watched for a time when no one was near to prevent her sad and dangerous employment, and succeeded in getting possession of the body of her loved brother, and placed it in a grave.

While the inhabitants of the more southern states had been suffering, those of Virginia had not been left to the enjoyment of peace; for the revengeful Arnold had been made a general in the English army, and was sent to invade the native state of Washington. Early in January he attacked Richmond, and succeeded in getting possession of it, and in destroying the military stores there. The resistance made to his power was too feeble to check him, and he used every opportunity for gratifying his desire to injure his countrymen.

All the events of that sad winter were such as caused the Americans to feel depressed

and increased the cares of Washington. There
were no sounds of gladness to hail the new
year of 1781, but it commenced with an event
that threatened ruin to the American cause.
That part of the army which was stationed
near Morristown, in New Jersey, had suffered
so much for want of clothing and food, that
they determined to march to Philadelphia
and force Congress to obtain supplies for
them, or else threaten that they would no
longer continue in service. Their commanding officer tried in vain to prevent their doing
so, and they marched towards Princeton.
Three officers, to whom the soldiers were attached, followed them to the place where they
encamped for the night, and prevailed on them
to send a sergeant from each regiment to meet
them and state their complaints, and what
they intended to demand form Congress.
They did so, and General Wayne, their commander, promised that their wishes should be
made known to Congress, and attended to ;
and urged them to return to their duty. General Washington was at that time at New
Windsor, on the North river, and General
Wayne immediately sent to him an account
of this alarming mutiny ; and of the demands
made by those who were engaged in it
Washington was much distressed by their
conduct ; but he felt that they had cause for
complaint, and thought that he ought not to go
to them lest they should disobey him, and

thus deserve a punishment which would prevent their being willing to return to duty. He made all the preparations that were possible for subduing them in case they became violent in their conduct; and directed General Wayne to inform Congress of what had happened, and let them endeavour to settle the business without his interference.

Congress appointed a committee to visit the camp of the mutineers, and make proposals to them, which after a short time they agreed to accept. The time for which a large portion of them had enlisted was passed, and they were discharged, so that the army was considerably reduced.

When Sir Henry Clinton heard of the mutiny, he immediately sent men to offer secretly to the revolters an assurance that he would receive them into his army, and supply all their wants, and would send a large force from New York to conduct them there in safety. But he had mistaken the feelings of the American soldiers. In a moment of extreme suffering they had yielded to the rash counsel of some impatient spirits, but no thought of becoming enemies of their country had entered their minds. They seized the messengers of Sir Henry, and made his proposals known to General Wayne, with an assurance that they had scorned them. The committee from Congress offered a reward to those who had made Sir Henry's messen-

gers prisoners, but they refused to accept it,
saying, " they had only done their duty, and
desired for the act nothing more than the approbation of their country, for which they had
so often fought and bled."

General Washington made use of this re-
volt to show to Congress, and to the different
states, the necessity of making more effectual
exertions to supply the army with clothing
and wholesome food. He represented their
sufferings so feelingly, that efforts were made
in each state, to contribute to their relief,
and small as the aid was, the sufferers were
satisfied with this proof, that their countrymen were not entirely unmindful of them.

When Congress had succeeded in satisfy-
ing the discontented troops, they became engaged in the interesting business of determining on a plan for a union of the different states
which would enable them to carry on the war
with less difficulty and expense. " Articles
of confederation," were drawn up, and in
February they were agreed to by all the members of Congress, and the knowledge of this
bond of union gave universal satisfaction.

All the accounts which General Washington heard from the southern states made him
very anxious to send more troops there.
The French fleet had been blocked up in
the harbour of Newport by an English fleet;
but a violent storm injured many of the English ships, and, by their being moved away

the French admiral was enabled to send out a few of his ships, which he directed to sail to the Chesapeake. When General Washington heard of this, he resolved to send troops immediately to Virginia, in the expectation that he could obtain aid from the French vessels in attacking some of the ports which were in possession of the English. The French ships soon returned to Newport, and in returning they captured an English frigate. General Washington was disappointed in his expectation of being aided by them at that time, but he sent troops, under the command of General Lafayette, to Virginia; and went to Newport to communicate to the French admiral a plan which he had formed for being assisted by some of his vessels. The admiral agreed to his proposals, and sent a part of his fleet out, but it was met by the English fleet, and, after a sharp action, they separated, and the French returned again to Newport.

A part of the troops which were marching to the south under the command of Lafayette, became discontented, and he discovered that every day some were secretly leaving him. He called together all that remained, and told them that he would not deceive them as to the difficulties and dangers to which he expected they would be exposed, for they were many; but, that any individual who was unwilling to encounter them, was at liberty to say so, and should have his permission to return to the army which they had left in New Jersey. This candid and generous conduct had the effect of stopping desertions; for the soldiers were ashamed to forsake so excellent a commander. In Baltimore he obtained, at his own expense, a variety of comforts for them, and the females of that city employed themselves immediately in making up summer clothing for them.

A large force had been sent from New York to Arnold, and Cornwallis had moved quickly to join him, and take command of all the troops. With so large a force, he was certain that he could readily defeat the little army of Lafayette, which he heard had entered Virginia, and he determined to attack it as soon as possible.

Lafayette wished to avoid Cornwallis, until he should have his force increased by some troops, which were on their way to join him, commanded by General Wayne. Cornwallis heard of this, and determined to prevent Lafayette receiving this aid, and was so confident of being successful, that he wrote, (with contempt for the youth of Lafayette,) in a letter which was intercepted, "the boy cannot escape me." But "the boy" moved with so much judgment and quickness, that his confident enemy was soon convinced that he could not overtake him, or prevent his being joined by the expected troops, and he gave up the pursuit, and determined to wait for his return.

When Lafayette received the additional
force, he turned, and was very soon within a
few miles of the camp of Cornwallis, who immediately suspected that he intended to attempt securing some military stores that had
been sent up the James river to Albemarle
Court-House, and he placed troops in a situation to attack him on the road which he supposed he would take. Lafayette thought that
Cornwallis would do so, and in the night
opened an old road, which had been long out
of use, by which he marched quietly to the
situation he wished to gain ; and in the morning, when Cornwallis thought to have him in
his power, he had the mortification of disco-
vering that he had passed by, and was placed
in a situation in which he could not be attacked with advantage. Cornwallis probably
thought that the American army was larger
than it really was ; for he gave up the intention he had formed of forcing it to an action, and marched to Williamsburgh. Lafayette followed him with great caution, and attacked some troops that were moving about
the country, but avoided the danger of an engagement with the main army.

In the rapid course of the English through
Virginia, they destroyed all the private property that came in their way, as well as that
which belonged to the public. Their ships
sailed up the rivers, and robbed the farms on
their borders. While they were thus employ-

ed in the Potomac, a message was sent from them to the farm of Washington, to demand a supply of provisions, with a threat that if they were not given, the buildings should be destroyed, and the farm laid waste. The person in whose care the farm had been left, was terrified by this threat, and went on board of one of the ships with some fresh provisions, to beg that the house might not be set on fire.

When General Washington received an account of this, he wrote to the person who had acted with so much impropriety, and told him, " I am sorry to hear of your losses, but that which gives me most concern is, that you should have gone on board of the vessels of the enemy, and furnished them with refreshments. It would have been a less painful circumstance to me, to have heard, that in consequence of your non-compliance with their request, they had burnt my house, and laid the plantation in ruins. You ought to have considered yourself as my representative, and should have reflected on the bad example of communicating with the enemy, and of making an offer of refreshment to them with a view to prevent a conflagration."

Lafayette acted with great prudence, and used every opportunity for preventing the enemy from plundering; but his force was too small to encounter the main body of their army, and he became very anxious that General Washington should go to Virginia, and give his aid to his native state, and free it from the destructive invaders. The government of the state also urged this very much; but Washington, considering America as his country, and making the safety of the whole country his object, would not suffer any love of his native state to change the plans which he thought would be most likely to produce benefit to the northern and middle, as well as the southern states. A sad gloom was spread over all of them when the year had commenced. The enemy were making preparations in Canada to march to Fort Pitt; and it was reported that they had assembled three thousand men, in ships on the lakes, to make an attack again from that quarter.

The dreaded Indians had united in large bands, and threatened all the western frontier with a renewal of their ferocious attacks.

The new troops, which Washington had expected from the different states, had not been raised, and those which had been long in service, were almost worn out with toils, and the want of necessary provision of food and clothing.

When any favourable event brightened the prospects of his country, Washington calmly rejoiced in it, but was not flattered into false security; and, when his countrymen were ready to despond, he could trust that the cheering beams of Divine favour would dis perse those clouds, and he became more ani·

mated and courageous as others became sad
and fearful. He continued to think, that to
get possession of New York would be of more
importance than any thing that he could venture to attempt, and he used every effort to
make preparations for doing so.

He formed a plan, which he communicated
to the French admiral, who was at Newport,
and who agreed to assist him in performing
it; and he earnestly urged to each state to
hasten the march of those troops which were
promised to him. All that depended on his
own exertions was performed with active perseverance; but the expected troops were delayed, and when they arrived, and he was
ready to execute his favourite plan, the French
admiral wrote to him, that he could not venture to take his heavy ships into New York
bay, and had resolved to sail for the Chesapeake; but there he could not remain long,
as he had been directed by his own government to return to the West Indies.

This information was severely trying to General Washington, as it disappointed his expectations of assistance from the fleet, and
obliged him to give up a plan which he was
ready to execute, and from which he hoped to
gain the most important success in freeing his
suffering country from its enemies.

Every one, who with piety notices the pro-
vidences of God, can know that our best blessings are often hid beneath our disappoint-

ments, as sweet flowers are concealed in bitter buds. Washington experienced this in the important results that followed his being obliged to bid farewell to all hopes of assistance in his cherished plan of attacking New York. He was unwillingly forced to form another, which proved far more advantageous to the interests of his country than that would have been.

Mr. (afterwards Judge) Peters, one of the board of war, was at the camp when the letter from the admiral was received; he said that General Washington gave it to him to read, and showed strong marks of anger; that he left him for a short time, and, on returning to him, he had cause to admire, as he often had done, how perfectly General Washington controlled his naturally hasty temper. He was as calm as if nothing had occurred to disturb him, and began immediately to form a new plan, without wasting the important moments in useless regrets. He determined on moving his army as quickly and secretly as possible to Virginia, before Sir Henry Clinton should suspect his design and send aid to Cornwallis.

When he informed Mr. Peters, and Mr. Robert Morris, the other commissioner of the board of war, who was at the camp, that his new plan was formed, and said, "What can you do for us under the present change of circumstances?' Mr. Peters said, "Inform me of the extent of your wants; I can do every thing with money,—nothing without it." As he said this, he looked at Mr. Morris, who said, " I understand you ;—I must have time to consider and calculate." They knew the difficulty of obtaining the money; and, when they had left Philadelphia, there was so little in the treasury chest, that Mr. Peters could not venture to take enough out of it to pay the expense of his journey to the camp. He returned to that city, and set to work industriously to prepare what General Washington had told him he should need.

In a very short time, almost two hundred pieces of artillery, and all the necessary ammunition, were prepared and sent off to Virginia. All the expense of this, as well as of the provision for, and pay of the troops, was defrayed by Mr. Morris, who gave notes for the promise of payment, to the amount of one million and four hundred thousand dollars, which were afterwards all paid.

General Washington informed Lafayette of his intention to come to Virginia, and desired him to do all in his power to prevent Cornwallis from saving himself by a sudden march to Charleston.

CHAPTER VIII

1781.

In South Carolina and Georgia the campaign of 1781 was a very active one.   A line
of posts had been continued by the English
from Charleston, in South Carolina, to Augusta, in Georgia.   General Sumpter and General Marion kept up a resistance, with a few
militia, and moved so quickly, that the English commander could not succeed in defeat-
ing them.   General Greene formed the bold
resolution of recovering Georgia.   He had
about eighteen hundred men, and his prospect
of procuring food for them was not very pro-
mising ; but he believed it to be for the interest of his country to make the attempt.   He
sent Colonel Lee with a detachment to join
Marion, and requested General Pickens to assemble the western militia of South Carolina,
and lay siege to Ninety-Six and Augusta
while he moved from his camp on Deep river
to Camden, where he arrived on the 19th
April.   Being unable to storm the works or
surround them, he encamped near Camden
with the hope of having some additional troops
of militia to aid him.   On the 25th April, he
had withdrawn his troops to Hobkirk's hill,
about a mile from Camden, and the English
general, Rawdon, marched out to attack him.
Although this attack was unexpected, the

Americans were soon ready to meet it, and
General Greene had every prospect of success, when his hopes were destroyed by one
of his regiments being thrown into confusion;
the English commander took advantage of this
with so much activity, that Greene soon perceived that to save his troops from a total defeat he must retreat, which he did to a place
about four miles from the field of battle. The
pursuit was only continued for three miles.

Colonel Lee had joined Marion in South
Carolina, and they attacked Fort Watson, on
the Santee river, and succeeded in obliging
the garrison to surrender.

A garrison had been placed in the dwelling
house of Mrs. Motte, situated on an eminence,
on the south side of the Congaree river, near
its junction with the Wateree; this was a
very important post, as all the provisions intended for the army at Camden were deposited there, and fortifications were thrown up
around the house. Marion and Lee determined to drive the garrison from this fortress,
and Lee informed Mrs. Motte, who was in
the neighbourhood, that they could not succeed without entirely destroying her house.
She replied, " The sacrifice of my property
is nothing; and I shall view its destruction
with delight, if it shall in any degree contribute to the good of my country." She then
gave him an Indian bow and arrows, which
had been kept as a curiosity in her family:

with these, lighted torches were shot upon
her house, which took fire, and thus the enemy were driven from it.   Lee then marched
against Fort Granby, on the Congaree, opposite the site of the town of Columbia, since
built there, and forced a garrison of three hundred and fifty men to surrender, while Marion
marched against Georgetown, on the Black
river, which place he reduced.

In July the intense heat of the climate made
it necessary for General Greene to give his
troops some rest, and he moved them to the
high hills of Santee for that purpose.   There
he was joined by some troops from North
Carolina.   In August he determined on once
more risking an action with the English army,
and, for that purpose, on the 22d, he proceeded to the Congaree, where he was joined by
General Pickens with the militia, and by
some state troops of South Carolina.   On
hearing of his approach, the English moved
to the Eutaw Springs, on the Santee, and
there, on the 8th September, a severe action
commenced, and was continued for some time
with great warmth and boldness on both sides.
At length the contest ceased, and both armies
claimed the victory.   In November the English retired to Charleston Neck, and to the
islands in the harbour.

When General Greene had entered South
Carolina, he found it completely conquered,
and defended by a regular army.   By a course

which was courageous, but prudent, he recovered the southern states, and, at the close of
the year 1781, they were again under their
own government. The rigour with which the
English exercised their power on those who
seemed disposed to resist, caused the war to
be more full of calamities to the inhabitants of
the southern states than those of any other
portion of the country.

At the north, still more important events
were taking place, as the summer advanced.
The movements of the American army were
such as to lead the enemy in New York
to think, that General Washington was preparing to attack that place; and Sir Henry
Clinton had no suspicion of his intention to
march to Virginia, until the army had crossed
the Delaware river, and it was then too late
for him to attempt to stop the progress of the
active troops.

With the hope of inducing Washington to
return for the defence of Connecticut, Sir
Henry sent to that state a strong detachment
of troops, in a fleet of transports; they were
commanded by Arnold, who had just returned
from Virginia.

The march of Washington was not prevented by this movement of the enemy, but
he advanced towards Virginia with all the
speed that was possible, and had the satisfaction of hearing, when he arrived in Chester,
early in September, that the French fleet was in

the Chesapeake. He gave directions to his officers to bring on the troops speedily, and went
himself to visit the admiral, and propose to him
a plan for an attack on the army of Cornwallis, in which he promised to assist him.

When Cornwallis had heard of the French
fleet appearing in the Chesapeake, he had
drawn all his troops together at Yorktown;
and with great activity and toil, they had
raised fortifications for their defence.

The town is situated on a strip of land,
about eight miles wide, between the James
and York rivers. Opposite to the town, on
the North side of York river, is Gloucester
Point, which projects into the river so as to
make it only one mile in width at that place.
Colonel Tarlton, with seven hundred men,
was posted on Gloucester Point. The southern banks of the river are high; some batteries
had been constructed on them by Virginia
troops, who had been stationed there some
time before. Cornwallis manned these batteries, and the main body of his army was encamped around Yorktown, within a range of
field works, raised for their defence.

The communication between Yorktown
and Gloucester Point, was defended by the
batteries on shore, and by several British
ships of war, which could ride in safety in
the broad and deep York river.

On the 25th of September, the last division
of Washington's army arrived at the landing

near Williamsburgh, on the James river.
They were allowed two days for rest, and on
the 28th, moved toward Yorktown. A detachment of French and American troops were
directed to watch and restrain Tarlton, and
the main body of the army was moved down
on the south side of the York river towards
Yorktown. The next day was employed in
preparing for the siege. General Lafayette
had joined Washington with the troops under
his command.

Washington displayed his military talent
and sound judgment in directing every movement that was to be made, and the siege was
carried on with great rapidity.

When the places of defence which the
English had raised at some distance from the
town were destroyed, and they were driven
back to seek for safety within the intrench-
ments which they had formed immediately
around it, Cornwallis finding himself so closely
pressed resolved to attempt escaping; and
during the night, he succeeded in sending several boats filled with troops across the York
river to Gloucester Point; but when these
troops were landed, a violent storm suddenly
arose, and drove the boats down the stream;
daylight began to dawn before they could be
recovered, and then it was necessary to use
them for the return of the few troops which
had been landed, as it was impossible to send
the rest of the army by the light of day, which

would show the movement to those Americans who were posted near Gloucester.

Being thus disappointed, and not having any reasonable cause for even a hope that he could save his army, Cornwallis wrote to General Washington to request that all hostilities might cease for twenty-four hours, during which time he would inform him on what terms he would surrender. Washington informed him that it was his ardent desire to spare the shedding of blood, and that he would listen with readiness to such terms as could be accepted; but requested that they might be made known immediately in writing, as he could quickly determine if he would agree to them.

Some of the proposals of Cornwallis, Washington could not consent to, and he wrote down the terms on which he expected him to surrender, and said he would not change them. These terms were; that all the army, with their arms and military stores, and all the ships and seamen, were to be delivered up. The troops to be prisoners of war to Congress, and the naval force to the French. The soldiers were to remain, with a few officers, in America; and the rest of the officers, were to be permitted to return to Europe on parole, or assurance from them that they would not serve again against the Americans. Cornwallis was to be allowed to send a ship unsearched to New York, to carry any papers which he chose to send there. These terms were accepted by the English general, and on the 19th of October, in the year 1781, the whole army of Cornwallis, which had been for so long a time the cause of distress and terror in the southern states, marched out of Yorktown, as prisoners of war. General Lincoln was appointed by General Washington to receive the submission of the conquered army, in the same manner in which Cornwallis had received his, and that of the American army, on the 12th of May, 1780, at Charleston.

While the troops of Cornwallis were marching out of the town, with cased colours and drums beating the sad sound of defeat, Washington said to his troops, " My brave fellows, let no sensation of satisfaction for the triumph you have gained, induce you to insult a fallen enemy ;—let no shouting—no clamourous huzzaing, increase their mortification. It is a sufficient satisfaction to us, that we witness their humiliation. Posterity will huzza for us !"

On the day after the surrender, he ordered that all who were under arrest should be set at liberty, and he closed his order with this direction—" Divine service shall be performed to-morrow in the different divisions of the army ; and the commander-in-chief recommends that all the troops that are not upon duty do assist at it, with a serious deportment, and that sensibility of heart, which the recollection of the surprising and particular interposition of Divine Providence in our favour, claims."

The capture of a formidable army, which had been moving with destructive power over more than eleven hundred miles of their country, was to the Americans a cause of heartfelt joy and thankfulness. The news was received at Philadelphia, then the seat of government, at night, and an aged watchman, who heard it, in the gladness of his heart, as he walked his round with a quick step, sung out, "Past one o'clock—and Cornwallis is taken!"

Congress heard the tidings with grateful sensations, and went in solemn procession to a place of worship, to return thanks to God for this deliverance from powerful foes; they also issued a proclamation, for "religiously observing through the United States the 13th day of December, as a day of thanksgiving and prayer."

CHAPTER IX.

1781—1787.

WHEN General Washington had performed all the duties which the surrender of Cornwal-

lis rendered necessary, before he could leave
Yorktown, he went to visit his respected and
aged mother, whom he had not seen for more
than six years. At the commencement of the
war he had removed her to the village of Fre-
dericksburg, where he thought she would be
comfortable, and distant from danger; and
from that time he had not been at liberty to
visit his native state, as his services were required by his country every day, and indeed
every moment. He was careful to send constantly to his parent, an account of himself
and the situation of public affairs, and she received all such intelligence with a confidence
in the wisdom of God, which prevented her
being depressed by the news of losses that frequently reached her ears. When she heard
of the success of her son in the December of
1777, (when he crossed the Delaware and
marched to Princeton,) she said, " George
appears to have deserved well of his country;" and, when her neighbours pressed
around her with letters that they had received,
full of his praises, she said, " Here is too much
flattery;—still George will not forget the lessons I early taught him;—he will not *forget
himself*, though he is the subject of so much
praise."

Washington knew that it would be no gratification to his good mother to see him surrounded by attendants, or to have his approach
made known by any kind of parade. He

therefore left the officers who rode with him, and dismounting from his horse, alone, and on foot, he went to her residence. When he entered it he found her usefully employed. As she embraced her son, she called him by an endearing name, which he well remember-ed she had always used when in his child-hood he deserved her approbation. She anxiously questioned him on the state of his health, talked of old times and old friends, but spoke not a word on the subject of his re-nown, or of the praise which his countrymen were giving him for his noble conduct.

When he left his revered parent, he went to his long forsaken home. Mrs. Washington was then there. She had been with him through each winter, and, as she said, had " heard the first cannon on the opening, and the last at the close of every campaign of the war."

When Washington was favoured with some success in any undertaking, he did not become less diligent in his efforts to complete it, and he wrote to General Greene, " I shall endea-vour to stimulate Congress to the best im-provement of our late success, by taking the most vigorous and effectual measures to be ready for an early and decisive campaign the next year."

He went to Philadelphia, and was success-ful in his wishes. In December, 1782, Con-gress passed resolutions which satisfied him

When he entered it, he found her usefully employed.

and he wrote to the different states to urge a
faithful compliance with these resolutions.
The army was placed in winter quarters, and
Washington became anxiously engaged in
preparations for the duties of the spring.

At the commencement of the year 1782,
there was not a dollar in the public treasury,
and, from the delay in collecting the taxes,
Washington knew that there could be no hope
of a supply for several months. Mr. Robert
Morris, the officer who superintended this business, wrote in great distress to Washington,
and said, " This candid state of my situation
and feelings I give to your bosom, because
you, who have already felt and suffered so
much, will be able to sympathize with me."

While Washington was using every effort
to hasten the collection of the money which
would be necessary for the subsistence of his
army, an account came from England that a
proposal had been made in Parliament to
make offers of peace. Washington had little
confidence in the probability of this proposi-
tion being agreed to by the English government, and he endeavoured to prevent his
countrymen being deceived into security by a
false expectation. Early in May, however,
an English commander, Sir Guy Carlton, arrived in New York, and wrote to Gen. Washington and to Congress, that Parliament had
determined on offering to conclude a peace, or
truce, with the *revolted colonies* of North

America; but, as no intimation was given that he had the power to propose any other terms than those which had been before rejected, Congress declined giving him a passport for himself and Admiral Digby, who, he informed Congress, were appointed to make known to them, in person, the resolutions of Parliament.

In August Sir Guy Carlton gave Washington the information that Parliament had sent a minister to Paris, who had the power to treat with all the parties at war, and that proposals for a general peace were then under consideration; and that the minister had been directed to offer, in the first place, that the independence of the " Thirteen Provinces" should be acknowledged.

The American commissioners, John Adams, Benjamin Franklin, John Jay, and Henry Laurens, who were in Paris, received the proposals for peace, and formed a treaty which satisfied every reasonable demand of America. This was signed on the 30th November, 1782, but it was not to be considered as entirely concluded, until a treaty should be formed between England and France, which was done on the 20th January, 1783.

When the American army had the expectation of soon being dismissed from service, they became anxious about the pay that was due to them, and which it was absolutely necessary they should receive, to enable them to re-

turn to their families. A very artful address
was circulated through the camp on the Hudson river, for the purpose of inducing them to
form some desperate resolutions to force the
government to a compliance with their demand
for payment. The address was accompanied
by an invitation to all the officers to meet on
the next day, and take the subject into consideration.   Washington was in camp, and his
firmness and judgment did not forsake him on
this important occasion. In his general orders he noticed the address, and expressed
his belief that the good sense of the officers
would prevent their " paying any attention to
such an irregular invitation," but invited them
to meet on another day, when, he said, they
could deliberate on what course they ought to
pursue.

Before that day arrived he conversed sepa-
rately with the officers, and used his influence
to lead them to adopt measures which he intended to propose. When they were assembled, he addressed them in a calm and affectionate manner; entreating them to disregard
the efforts that were made to induce them to act
disgracefully, and assuring them of his confidence that Congress would treat them justly.

This address from one whom they loved
and had been accustomed to obey,—in whose
judgment and affection they had perfect confidence, could not fail to influence the army,
and the officers immediately formed resolu-

tions which satisfied their anxious commander, and proved the strength of their respect
for his advice. It has been said that "perhaps, in no instance, did the United States re
ceive from heaven a more signal deliverance
through the hands of Washington, than in the
termination of this serious transaction." His
conduct gave a new proof of the kindness of
his heart, soundness of his judgment, and pu-
rity of the love of his country. He wrote to
Congress an account of what had occurred;
and earnestly entreated that the just demands
of the army might be immediately attended to,
and that provision might be made for a further compensation than a mere pay which was
due to the officers. He said, "if (as has been
suggested for the purpose of inflaming their
passions,) the officers of the army are to be
the only sufferers by this revolution; if retiring
from the field they are to grow old in poverty,
wretchedness and contempt, and owe the miserable remnant of that life to charity, which
has hitherto been spent in honour, then shall
I have learned what ingratitude is; then shall
I have realized a tale which will imbitter every
moment of my future life."

Congress received a petition from the officers, and then formed a resolution, that in addition to the pay due to them, they should
receive full pay for five years; but they knew
it would be some time before the money could
be raised. The officers were satisfied with

the promise, and in the course of the summer
a large portion of the troops returned to their
homes.

A few new recruits, who were stationed at
Lancaster, marched to Philadelphia and placed
sentinels at the doors of the State House,
where Congress were sitting, and threatened
to attack them if their demands for pay were
not granted within twenty minutes. They
did not perform their threat, but kept Congress prisoners for three hours.

When General Washington heard of this
outrage, he sent fifteen hundred men to quell
the mutineers, but this had been done without
any blood being shed before the troops arrived.
He wrote to Congress that he felt much distressed on hearing of the insult which had
been offered by these " soldiers of a day ;"
and contrasted their conduct with that of the
soldiers who had "borne the heat and burden
of the war ; veterans," he said, " who have
patiently endured nakedness, hunger and cold ;
who have suffered and bled without a murmur,
and who, with perfect good order have retired
to their homes without a settlement of their
accounts, or a farthing of money in their pock-
ets. We are as much astonished at the virtues
of the latter, as we are struck with horror and
detestation at the proceedings of the former."
In consequence of the insult, Congress adjourned, to meet at Princeton, in New Jersey,
in the close of the month of June, 1783. They

sat there in the Library room of the College for about three months; and then adjourned to meet at Annapolis, in Maryland.

The seeds of freedom which had been sown in weakness, and guarded with toil through eight years, produced a rich harvest in the blessings of *independence* and *peace*, which spread quickly over the United States; and every American heart had cause to say, with humble gratitude, to the Great Ruler of events, "O thou that savest by thy right hand them that put their trust in thee, from those that rise up against them—thou hast been our helper."

When General Washington had proclaimed to his army on the 19th of April, the tidings of a universal peace, he said, "on such a happy day, which is the harbinger of peace; a day which completes the eight years of the war, it would be ingratitude not to rejoice, it would be insensibility not to participate in the general felicity;" and he directed that the Chaplains, with their several brigades, should "render thanks to Almighty God for all his mercies, particularly for his overruling the wrath of man to his own glory; and causing the rage of war to cease among the nations." When he dismissed the troops from service on the 2d of November, he gave them serious and affection ate advice as to their future conduct; and assured them that he should recommend them to their grateful country, and in his prayers "to the

God of armies." Earnestly desiring that his countrymen might secure a continuance of the favour of heaven, he wrote an address to the governors of the different states, which address he said he wished them to consider as " the legacy of one who had ardently desired on all occasions to be useful to his country ; and who, even in the shade of retirement, would not fail to implore the divine benediction upon it." The address contained important and wise counsel, and he concluded it with the assurance, " I now make it my earnest prayer, that God would have you and the state over which you preside, in his holy protection, and that he would incline the hearts of the citizens to cultivate a spirit of subordination, and obedience to government, and to entertain a brotherly affection and love for one another ; for their fellow citizens of the United States at large, and particularly for their brethren who have served in the field ; and finally, that he would be most graciously pleased to dispose us all to do justice, to love mercy, and to demean ourselves with that charity, humility, and pacific temper of mind, which were the characteristics of the Divine Author of our blessed religion ; without an humble imitation of whose example in these things we can never hope to be a happy nation."

In November all the English troops left New York, and General Washington entered it accompanied by Governor Clinton and a number of American officers. Many Americans from distant places visited New York, to unite with their countrymen there in public expressions of joy; one of this number was General Washington's nephew, Bushrod Washington, then a youth, and afterwards an eminent and highly respected Judge, of the Supreme court of the United States. The following anecdote connected with that visit, he kindly communicated for this biography, in a letter dated Mount Vernon, June 1st 1829. "In the early part of the year 1782 I was sent by my father to Philadelphia, for the purpose of prosecuting the study of law. It was my good fortune to meet General Washington there. Within a few days after my arrival, but not until he had placed me in the office of Mr. Wilson, and secured for me the countenance and kind attention of some of his friends in that city, he returned to the state of New York. Upon that occasion, or at a subsequent period, (I cannot now recollect which,) he requested me to make inquiries respecting a kind of cloth which he particularly described, and wished to purchase, and to inform him by letter the price, and where it was to be procured. I readily promised an early compliance with this request, and intended, I doubt not, at the time, conscientiously to fulfil my engagement. I postponed doing so, however, from day to day, until the subject was for gotten altogether; or was too seldom thought of, to leave more than a very slight impression upon my mind. About the time when the evacuation of New York, by the British troops was to be commemorated in that city, the General wrote to me, giving me permission to be present on that occasion, and enclosing me money for my expenses. On my arrival in New York, I called at his lodgings, and was received by him with his former kindness. After some general conversation, he asked me if I had attended to his request respecting the cloth, and what had been the result of my inquiries? My feelings, at that moment, may be imagined, —it is not in my power to describe them. I had no excuse to offer, and as soon as the power of speech was allowed me, I acknowledged my delinquency. Turning to me with a mildness which I did not deserve, but with an impressiveness in his manner which I have never forgotten, he observed, " *remember, young man, never in future to make a promise, even of a trivial kind, the nature and extent of which you have not duly considered; having made it, let nothing prevent a punctual performance of it, if it be within your power.*" He then dismissed me without an additional reproach or observation."

General Washington remained in New York, until December, and when the day arrived on which he had determined to leave it, the officers of the army assembled to bid him farewell. When their loved commander en-

tered the room in which they were, he could
not speak for several moments ; but, when he
had calmed his strong feelings, he said " with
a heart, full of love and gratitude, I now take
leave of you ; I most devoutly wish that your
latter days may be as prosperous and happy
as your former have been honourable. I cannot come to each of you to take my leave, but
shall be obliged to you if each of you will
come and take me by the hand."   General
Knox, who was nearest to him, turned, and
Washington took his hand, and then put his
arms around him, and in the same affectionate manner embraced each officer.   A tear
from the heart filled every eye ; but no word
could be uttered to break the silence of the
affecting scene.   Washington left the room,
and the officers followed him in noiseless procession, and with sad countenances to the
boat which was to convey him away from
them. Washington stepped into the boat, and
turning towards the shore waved his hat without speaking ; the officers returned the same
last farewell, and continued to gaze after their
beloved commander until they could no longer distinguish his form, and then they returned in sadness to the place where they had
assembled.

Washington could not enjoy rest until he
had performed all the duties which his upright mind dictated, and he proceeded to Philadelphia to give an account of the manner in

which he had expended the public money. All his accounts were written by himself, and every entry made in the most exact manner, so as to give the least trouble in comparing them with the receipts which accompanied them. He made no charge for his services, but had spent a considerable portion of his own fortune. The regularity and minuteness with which he had kept an account of every sum received and expended during eight years, and the faithfulness with which he had, in the midst of his many employments, attended to having the public money used in the most economical and advantageous manner, proved that he had a right to the noble title of *an honest man.* If he had not merited that, all his former titles would have been without value. From Philadelphia he proceeded to Annapolis, where Congress was sitting, and there he proved that he was a patriot, by giving back the power which had been placed in his hands, when he could no longer use it for the benefit of his country. Congress appointed the 23d December for receiving his resignation, and a crowd of spectators witnessed the interesting ceremony. He was received by Congress as the "founder and guardian of the republic." Feeling the importance of the blessings of freedom and peace which the Great Ruler of the universe had made Washington an agent to obtain for them, they looked at him, when about to re-

sign his power, with emotions of admiration
and gratitude; and recollecting how closely
they had been connected with him in scenes
of distress and danger, there were few eyes
unwet with a tear. With unambitious dignity
he rose and addressed General Mifflin, the
President of Congress. He said, "I resign
with satisfaction the appointment I accepted
with diffidence; a diffidence in my abilities to
accomplish so arduous a task, which, however, was superseded by a confidence in the
rectitude of our cause, the support of the supreme power of the union and the patronage
of heaven. The successful termination of the
war has verified the most sanguine expectations; and my gratitude for the interposition
of Providence, and the assistance I have received from my countrymen, increases with
every review of the momentous contest. * * *
I consider it as an indispensable duty to close
this last act of my official life, by commending
the interests of our dearest country to the protection of Almighty God, and those who have
the superintendence of them to his holy keeping. Having now finished the work assigned
me, I retire from the great theatre of action,
and bidding an affectionate farewell to this
august body, under whose orders I have so
long acted, I here offer my commission, and
take my leave of all the employments of public
life." He then gave his commission to the
President, who, when he had received it, an-

swered him in the name of Congress, and said, " Having defended the standard of liberty in this new world : having taught a lesson useful to those who inflict, and to those who feel op-pression, you retire from the great theatre of action with the blessings of your fellow-citizens; but the glory of your virtues will not terminate with your military command; it will continue to animate remotest ages.   We join you in commending the interests of our dearest country to the protection of Almighty God, beseeching him to dispose the hearts and minds of its citizens to improve the opportunity afforded to them of becoming a happy and respectable nation.   And for you, we address to Him our earnest prayers, that a life so beloved may be fostered with all his care ; that your days may be as happy as they have been illustrious ; and that he will finally give you that reward-which this word cannot give."

History presents no more elevated scene than that of a successful hero, at the close of a long war, giving up his command, and a nation, just having achieved its independence, in the solemn act of dissolving its military state, all uniting in ascribing praise to that God whose kind Providence they had enjoyed, and commending each other to his protection in time, and his favour throughout eternity.

When Washington had thus resigned the title of " Commander-in-chief," he took that of private citizen, and retired to his peaceful home. The satisfaction he felt in doing so was expressed in a letter to his friend, Lafayette, who had returned to France soon after the surrender of Cornwallis. Washington wrote to him, "At length I have become a private citizen, on the banks of the Potomac, and under the shade of my 'own vine and my own fig-tree,' and free from the bustle of a camp and the busy cares of public life. I have not only retired from all public employments, but am retiring within myself, and shall be able to view the solitary walk, and tread the paths of private life, with heartfelt satisfaction."

To General Knox he thus addressed himself:—"I feel now, as I conceive a weary traveller must do, who, after treading many a painful step, with a heavy burden on his shoulders, is eased of the latter, having reached the haven to which all the former were directed,—and from his house-top, in looking back and tracing with eager eye, the meanders by which he has escaped the quicksands and mires which lay in his way, and into which none but the all-powerful Guide and Dispenser of human events, could have prevented his falling."

For several months after his return home, he received, almost every day, addresses from all parts of the union, expressing the affection and gratitude of his countrymen. He deserved this and no doubt was gratified by it; but the praise of man had no ill effect on his modest mind For a little time, when he awoke in the morning, he would forget that he was in his peaceful home, and, as he had been accustomed to do, would begin to think of what orders he should give his army, or what public business he should transact during the day; but he soon interested himself in the cultivation of his farm, and in assisting his neighbours to improve theirs; and for this purpose he wrote to England to obtain the best information of all the improvements which were discovered there in agriculture.

When the English ceased to act as enemies of his country, Washington did not cherish against them feelings of resentment. His liberal mind was willing to acknowledge their national greatness and usefulness, and his heart was one that could estimate the virtues of those individuals of the nation who have devoted their lives to the promotion of the temporal and eternal interests of their fellow beings.

He travelled for a short time through those parts of his country with which he was unacquainted, and, on his return, said he had new cause for acknowledging " the goodness of that Providence which has dealt his favours to us with so profuse a hand." He was desirous that these gracious gifts should not be neglected, and he formed plans for improving the navigation of some of the extensive rivers which flow through this country. He said he considered the extension of inland navigation as " an effectual means of cementing the union of the states." His plan was that the navigation of the eastern waters should be extended, and communicate with the western; that these again should be opened from the Ohio to Lake Erie. Since his death his design has been extensively executed, and, by its constantly increasing advantages, proving the excellence of his foresight and wisdom. He succeeded in having two companies formed for improving the James and Potomac rivers. On this occasion the legislature of Virginia subscribed for the same number of shares for Washington, in each company, that were to be taken for the state; but, when informed of this, he assured them that he must decline accepting it, as he had determined never to change the resolution he had formed when he entered into public service, "to shut his hand against every pecuniary recompense;" but he proposed to the legislature that the shares intended for him should be given to some public institution, and they were given to two schools; one of which was near the Potomac, and the other near James river.

General Lafayette again crossed the ocean, and visited Mount Vernon, and no doubt passed some interesting hours with his friend Washington. But those hours of social enjoy-

ment were few, for these friends were soon
again engaged in public scenes and cares. Before Lafayette returned to France he visited
the mother of Washington, to bid her farewell
and ask her blessing. She received him kind
ly, and talked with him of the happy pros
pects of her country, and of the conduct of
her virtuous son, whom Lafayette praised with
the warmth of strong attachment.

She listened calmly to him, and then replied, *" I am not surprised at what George
has done, for he was always a very good
boy."*

On leaving this venerable woman, Lafayette
asked and received her blessing, and bade her
a last farewell. When he took leave of his
friend, he indulged a lively hope that they
would once more meet; but when again he
visited America, he was received as the " Nation's Guest," and, instead of being welcomed
to Mount Vernon by the smiles of Washington, he was led to his tomb to shed tears of
sorrow.

Desiring anxiously that his native country
should be freed from the tyrannical government which oppressed it, Lafayette felt a deep
interest in the revolution which soon commenced in France; but his heart must have
been pained by the manner in which it was
conducted. In the attempt to throw off the
oppression of man, the restraints of morality
were cast away, and the human passions raged

uncontrolled. The consequences were dread
ful ; the tenderest ties of nature were disregarded,—the truths of religion were denied,
and the worship of God abolished. So that
whilst this country, which looked to the Divine blessing for liberty, received it, France
has ever since that time been unsettled and
unhappy, and often the scene of civil war and
bloodshed.

Young Americans ! as you grow up to manhood, and enjoy the great blessing of freedom
from all unjust and oppressive laws of man,
beware of wishing to be free from the just and
righteous laws of your Creator, lest you bring
upon yourselves as a nation, the displeasure of
him whose " kingdom is an everlasting kingdom," and whose "dominion endureth throughout all generations." To those who will not
obey him, he has said, " I will bring evil upon
this people, even the fruit of their thoughts,
because they have not hearkened unto my
word, nor to my law, but have rejected it."
While you are exercising what you call liberty of conscience, remember the assurance
of him who " taught as one having authority :"
" If ye *continue in my word* ye shall know
the *truth*, and the *truth* shall make you *free ;*
verily, verily, I say unto you, whosoever com-
mitteth *sin* is the *servant* of sin." If Christ
" shall make you free, ye shall be free indeed."

CHAPTER X

1787—1789.

AFTER the Americans obtained independence, those who thought wisely on public affairs were soon convinced that the " Articles of Confederation," which had united the states in time of war, would not bind them together in harmony under one government in time of peace.

Congress had borrowed money from the French nation during the war, and they were also in debt to the officers of the army, and to other Americans; and were unable to pay even the interest of the money due, because they did not possess the power to tax the people, or to lay duties on imported goods.

The advice of Washington at the close of the war had been too soon forgotten. He had said then to his countrymen, "The path of duty is plain before us. Let us as a nation be just; let us fulfil the public contracts, which Congress had undoubtedly a right to make for the purpose of carrying on the war, with the same good faith we suppose ourselves bound to perform our private engagements."

From his retirement he watched with interest the conduct of his countrymen, and began to feel alarmed lest they should disgrace themselves as a nation. He corresponded on the subject with the wise American patriots, who used all their influence to convince the people that it was necessary for the credit and prosperity of their country, to give more power to Congress and to strengthen the bond of union. There was a great variety of opinions on the subject, but at length all the states, except Rhode Island, agreed to choose members for a convention to plan a better form of national government. Virginia placed Washington first on the list of members.

On the second Monday in May, 1787, the Convention met at Philadelphia, and chose Washington its president; and, after long and serious consultation on the important subject, that Constitution was formed under which, by the favour of a gracious Providence, the United States have become so prosperous, and the American nation so happy and respectable. The opinions of the members of the Convention seemed to be so opposed to each other on some points, that it was feared they could agree on no plan that would suit the whole country. The debate was increasing in warmth, when Dr. Franklin, with his accustomed wisdom and coolness, endeavoured to promote harmony by proposing an adjournment for three days, that there might be time for serious consideration of the subject. He concluded his speech to the following effect:—

" The small progress we have made, after four or five weeks close attendance and conti-

nued reasoning with each other, our different
sentiments on almost every question, several
of the last producing as many *noes* as *ayes,*
is, methinks, a melancholy proof of the im-
perfection of the human understanding. We,
indeed, seem to *feel* our want of political wisdom, since we have been running all about in
search of it. We have gone back to ancient
history for models of government, and examined the different forms of those republics
which, having been originally formed with the
seeds of their own dissolution, now no longer
exist : and we have viewed modern states all
round Europe, but find none of their constitu-
tions suitable to our circumstances.

"In this situation of this assembly, groping
as it were in the dark to find political truth, and
scarcely able to distinguish it when presented
to us, how has it happened, sir, that we have
not hitherto once thought of humbly applying
to the Father of Light to illuminate our under-
standings?—In the beginning of the contest
with Britain, when we were sensible of danger, we had daily prayers in this room for
Divine protection. Our prayers, sir, were
heard ;—and they were graciously answered.
All of us, who were engaged in the struggle,
must have observed frequent instances of a
superintending Providence in our favour. To
that kind Providence we owe this happy opportunity of consulting in peace on the means
of establishing our future and national felicity.

And have we now forgotten that powerful
Friend? Or do we imagine we no longer
need his assistance? I have lived, sir, a long
time; and the longer I live, the more con-
vincing proofs I see of this truth, *that God
governs in the affairs of men*. And if a sparrow cannot fall to the ground without his notice, is it probable that an empire can rise
without his aid?—We have been assured, sir,
in the sacred writings, that "except the Lord
build the house, they labour in vain that build
it." I firmly believe this; and I also believe,
that without his concurring aid, we shall succeed in this political building no better than
the builders of Babel: we shall be divided by
our little, partial, local interests; our projects
will be confounded; and we ourselves shall
become a reproach and a by-word down to
future ages. And, what is worse, mankind
may hereafter, from this unfortunate instance,
despair of establishing government by human
wisdom, and leave it to chance, war, and conquest. I therefore beg leave to move,

" That henceforth prayers, imploring the
assistance of Heaven, and its blessing on
our deliberations, be made in this assembly
every morning before we proceed to business;
and that one or more of the clergy of this city
be requested to officiate in that service."

One member only opposed this motion, and
a person who was present relates, that whilst
he was making his objections, Washington

fixed his eye upon him with an expression of mingled surprise and indignation. No one condescended to notice the opposition, and the proposal was at once carried by the votes of all the other members. The adjournment, also, according to his suggestion, took place, and, after the Convention had been opened with prayer, when they met again, Dr. Franklin stated the necessity and equity of mutual concessions from all parts of the Union. His views were adopted, and the important business, on which they were so warm when they separated, was soon despatched, and the whole constitution at length agreed to. The people have preserved this, their own chosen constitution, for more than fifty years, and have seen their happiness, prosperity and renown, grow with its growth, and strengthen with its strength. How firmly should every American delight to cherish a union which has been so blessed by the God of nations, and ardently desire that " the flag of the republic, now known and honoured throughout the earth, may continue to float over the sea and over the land, without one stripe erased or polluted, or a single star obscured."

The constitution was signed by the delegates from twelve states, on the 17th September, 1787, and, when made known to the people, they were of one opinion, that Washington was the man most worthy to be the President of the United States. One of his

friends, Colonel Lee, who had an opportunity
of hearing the wishes which were universally
expressed by his countrymen, wrote to Washington, to entreat that he would not suffer his
love of private life to prevent his consenting
to engage again in public duties; and added,
" If the same success should attend your efforts on this important occasion which has distinguished you hitherto, then to be sure you
will have spent a life which Providence rare-
ly, if ever, gave to the lot of one man."

Elections were held throughout the United
States, and, when the votes were opened and
counted in the Senate, it was found that Washington was unanimously elected.

On the 14th April, 1789, the fifty-seventh
year of his age, Congress informed him of his
appointment, and he accepted it, because it
was the call of his countrymen to serve them.
On this occasion he wrote to one of his friends
his sentiments on this subject, which showed
the dignity and modesty of his character; he
said, " I am unwilling in the evening of a
life, nearly consumed in public cares, to quit
a peaceful abode for an ocean of difficulties,
without the competency of political skill, abilities, and inclination, which are necessary to
manage the helm. I am sensible that I am
embarking the voice of the people and a good
name of my own, on this voyage ; but what
returns will be made for them, Heaven alone
can foretell,—integrity and firmness are all I

can promise; these, be the voyage long or
short, shall never forsake me, although I may
be deserted by all men; for of the consolations
which are to be derived from these, under
any circumstances, the world cannot deprive
me."

He visited his respected mother to inform
her of his appointment. He had endeavoured
to prevail on her to make Mount Vernon the
home of her latter years; but she would not
consent to leave her humble dwelling, which
was particularly dear to her from having near
it a rural spot, made private by surrounding
rocks and trees, where she daily offered to
her Creator her confessions and prayers.
When her son told her he must bid her farewell, he said, "As soon as the weight of public business, which must necessarily attend
the outset of a new government, can be disposed of, I shall return to Virginia, and"—
"You will see me no more," said his mother,
interrupting him, "My great age warns me,
that I shall not be long in this world,—I trust
in God that I may be somewhat prepared for
a better. Go, George, go my son! and perform your duties, and may the blessing of
God, and that of a mother, be with you always." She cast her arms around his neck,
and resting his head on the shoulder of his
aged parent, the truly great man shed tears
of filial tenderness.

He parted from her with the sad feeling,

that he should indeed see her no more, and in a short time, these painful apprehensions were realized. She was eighty-five years old at the time of her death; and was buried near Fredericksburgh, Va. Over her grave, a gentleman of New York has lately placed a noble monument, on which is only this inscription:

MARY,

THE MOTHER OF WASHINGTON.

In the middle of April, Washington was called by duty to bid farewell to his farm. He set off for New York, the seat of government, and in the journal, which it was his custom to keep, he wrote at the close of that day, thus: "About ten o'clock I bade adieu to Mount Vernon, to private life, and to domestic felicity, and with a mind oppressed with more anxious and painful sensations than I have words to express, set out for New York, —with the best dispositions to render service to my country in obedience to its call, but with less hope of answering its expectations."

His neighbours and the citizens of Alexandria assembled, and met him on the road to attend him to that place, where they invited him to eat a parting dinner with them. When he was leaving them to proceed on his journey, they said in their affectionate address to him, "Again your country commands your care. The first, the best of citizens, must leave us. Our aged must lose their ornament,—our youth, their model,—our agriculture, its improver,—our commerce, its friend, —our academy, its protector,—our poor, their benefactor. Farewell! Go, and make a grateful people happy.—To that Being, who maketh and unmaketh at his will, we commend you; and after the accomplishment of the arduous business to which you are called, may he restore to us again the best of men, and the most beloved fellow-citizen."

After thanking them for their expressions of kindness, Washington said, in reply,— "The whole tenor of my life has been open to your inspection; and my past actions, rather than my present declarations, must be the pledge of my future conduct. All that now remains for me, is to commit myself and you to the protection of that beneficent Being, who on a former occasion, hath happily brought us together, after a long and distressing separation. Perhaps the same gracious Providence will again indulge me. Unutterable sensations must then be left to more expressive silence; while from an aching heart I bid you all, my affectionate friends and kind neighbours, farewell."

He wished his journey to be private; but preparations were made in every town and village through which he was to pass, to give him proofs of the gratitude of his countrymen for his past services, and of their confidence, that his future ones would be blessings to them.

Philadelphia was illuminated, and the next day he was welcomed to Trenton with joy. On the bridge over the Assumpinck Creek, an arch had been erected, and ornamented with laurels and flowers, and it was supported by thirteen pillars, entwined with wreaths of evergreen. On the front of the arch was inscribed, in large letters, the date of the first battle of Trenton, and of the day on which the American troops had made a bold stand on the borders of the Assumpinck, by which the progress of the English army had been stopped. Under this was written, "The defender of the mothers will be the protector of the daughters." As he left his carriage to walk over the bridge, a company of young girls went before him, and strewed fresh flowers in his path.

At Elizabethtown a committee from Congress received him, and conducted him to the Point, where he entered a handsome boat, that had been prepared to convey him to New York.

His return to that city was not in silence, as his departure from it had been; and in his journal he remarked, that the decorations of the ships, the music in the boats, the roar of the cannon, and the acclamations of the people, filled him with sensations not more pleasing than painful, as he thought how changed the scene might be " after all his labours to do good."

The 30th day of April was appointed for taking the solemn oath with which the constitution requires the president to commence the duties of his important office. In the morning of that day, the clergymen of the city met their congregations, to unite in offering prayers to God for his blessing on the people, and the president whom they had chosen.

The oath was administered by R. R. Livingston, Chancellor of the state of New York, and the interesting ceremony was witnessed by a great concourse of people, for it was performed in an open gallery adjoining the senate chamber, and fronting Broad street. All stood in solemn silence, until the oath was taken, and then, when the Chancellor proclaimed that GEORGE WASHINGTON WAS THE PRESIDENT OF THE UNITED STATES, a shout of joy burst from many thousands of grateful and affectionate hearts. The president went into the senate chamber, and in a modest but dignified manner, addressed the senate and house of representatives.

In the course of his address he said, " It will be peculiarly improper to omit, in this first official act, my fervent supplications to that Almighty Being, who rules over the universe,—who presides in the councils of nations, and whose providential aid can supply every human defect,—that his benediction

may consecrate to the liberties and happiness
of the people of the United States, a government instituted by themselves for these essen-
tial purposes,—and may enable every instrument employed in its administration to execute
with success the functions allotted to his
charge. In tendering this homage to the great
Author of every public and private good, I
assure myself that it expresses your sentiments not less than my own ; nor those of
my fellow-citizens at large, less than either.
No people can be bound to acknowledge and
adore the invisible hand which conducts the
affairs of men, more than the people of the
United States. Every step by which they
have advanced to the character of an independent nation, seems to have been distinguished
by some token of providential agency."

In conclusion, he said, " I shall take my
present leave, but not without resorting once
more to the benign Parent of the human race,
in humble supplication, that since he has been
pleased to favour the American people with
opportunities for deliberating in perfect tranquillity, and dispositions for deciding with
unparalleled unanimity on a form of govern
ment for the security of their union and ad-
vancement of their happiness ; so his divine
blessing may be equally conspicuous, in the
enlarged views, the temperate consultations
and wise measures, on which the success of
this government must depend."

The Senate, in reply, expressed their high estimation of his wisdom and virtue, and said, "All that remains is that we join in your fervent supplications for the blessing of Heaven on our country ; and that we add our own for the choicest of those blessings on the most beloved of her citizens." The important ceremony of that day was closed with divine worship.

When Washington entered on the public duties of his office, he did not forget that judicious regulations were needful for the government of his own household. He made rules for his family, which every member knew must not be disregarded. He directed that an account should be given to him every week of the money that was expended. He wished to entertain with generous hospitality all visiters whom it was proper to receive, but he would not permit any needless expense. In making regulations for his family he remembered the Sabbath ; he always attended a place of worship, and was not in the custom of receiving any visiters, except Mr. Trumbull, who was then Speaker of Congress, and afterwards the Governor of Connecticut. He was in the habit of spending an hour with the President on every Sabbath evening, and was so regular in the time of his visit, that the servants, by looking at the clock, knew to a moment when to be ready to open the door to the " speaker's bell," as they called the door bell on sunday evening, because no other hand than his then rung it.

The president did not return any visits, and appointed certain hours of two days in the week, for being visited by persons who had no business to transact with him. In the performance of his duties, the president set an example of punctuality, and by the strictest regard to it, in the smallest as well as the greatest concerns, gave a plain and excellent lesson on the *value of time, and importance of truth.* In making an appointment he named the exact time, that not one moment might be wasted in the idleness which uncertainty in this respect often occasions. All his promises were given with " the lip of truth," therefore he was punctual to a moment in performing them. He required punctuality in every member of his household, and was once heard to say, to a visiter, who had come late to dinner, " Our cook never asks if the company has come, but if the hour has come." He had fixed on a convenient hour for members of Congress and other invited guests to dine with him, and being careful to have the clock which stood in his entry exactly right, he allowed five minutes for the difference in clocks and watches, and after that time did not wait for any person. If some forgetful or lagging guest came after the time, the president usually made some such remark as " We are too punctual for you." When Congress met in Philadelphia, he appointed the hour of twelve for attending and delivering his speeches to them, and he always entered the state-house, where Congress sat, when the state-house clock was striking the hour. The lesson on punctuality, which the great Washington taught by his own practice, should be particularly attended to by the young. Their hours should be devoted to improvement, and dreadful is the waste, it they are spent in an improper manner. The sacred hours of the sabbath should be accounted particularly precious, and every opportunity of instruction they afford should be attended to with care and punctuality.

CHAPTER XI.

1789—1796.

ALL the important business attending the commencement of the new government was conducted with wisdom. When Congress adjourned, the president prepared to visit New England; on the 15th October he began his journey, and, passing through Connecticut and Massachusetts, went as far as Portsmouth, in New Hampshire; returning by a different route to New York. He had a favourable opportunity for observing the improvements of the important portion of his country through which he travelled, and was in every place received with proofs of joy and attachment.

At Cambridge, the governor and council of Massachusetts met him, and accompanied him to Boston ; the selectmen received him at the entrance of the town, and a procession of the inhabitants was formed, which extended to the state-house, and he noticed with satisfaction the children, who made a part of the procession, conducted by their teachers. A triumphal arch was erected, and over it, on one side, was the inscription, "To the man who unites all hearts ;" and on the opposite side, "To Columbia's favourite son."

The president returned to New York, and Congress again met on the 8th January, 1790. They passed several acts of importance, and then determined that the seat of government should be removed to Philadelphia. This session of Congress continued until the 12th August, when they adjourned. The health of the president had been injured by his close attention to public business, and he thought that a visit to Mount Vernon would refresh and strengthen him. He wished to travel as privately as possible, but, when he thought that he was approaching the villages without being noticed, the villagers were ready to give him some proof of a joyful welcome ; and supposing the probable time for his return, the school children were promised by their teachers that they should see Washington, which they thought was a high reward for diligence.

After a short indulgence in the enjoyment of rural sights and sounds, the president returned from Mount Vernon to meet Congress at Philadelphia. One important subject which engaged Congress at that session, was war with the Indians.

As early as the year 1736, Moravian missionaries, taking no weapon but " the sword of the Spirit, which is the word of God," visited the Indians, and carried to them " the glad tidings of great joy which shall be to all people." They preached " Jesus Christ and him crucified ;" and many of the wild rangers of the forest listened to the sound of the Gospel, and, with some of their most ferocious chieftains, submitted to its peaceful rules. All such formed settlements, cultivated the ground around them, and made spots in the wilderness to " blossom like the rose." One of those settlements in Pennsylvania was called Nain. A young Nanticoke Indian visited it, and remained there for a month; on being taken ill afterwards, he called two of his brothers to him, and said to them, " in Nain they teach the right way to eternal life. There I have heard that our Creator became a man, died on the cross for our sins, was buried, rose again, and went into heaven, and that whosoever believes in him shall not perish; but, when he dies, shall live with him for ever. If you wish to hear these good words go to Nain." He died, praying with his last breath for pardon, and his brothers both went to Nain to hear "the good words" which he had received with faith and joy. Though the power of the Gospel was thus felt, and proved by the changed conduct of many of the Indians, yet their number was few compared with that of those who still roamed through the forests, and took advantage of every opportunity for attacking the inhabitants of the frontiers. Washington being well acquainted with the cruel manner in which the Indians conducted their attacks, knew the sufferings to which his countrymen on the frontiers were exposed; and as he was never satisfied with merely feeling a sympathy in the distresses of his fellow-beings, he used every means in his power to relieve them. He earnestly recommended to Congress to endeavour to form treaties with the Indians. He was "for peace," but the Indians were "for war." Troops were sent out against them, commanded by General Harmar, but these troops were defeated, in a battle near Chilicothe. Congress then gave the president the means of raising another army, and General Arthur St. Clair was appointed to the command of it.

After the president had made all the necessary arrangements for recruiting the army, he paid a visit to the southern states, and in passing through them, received the same proofs of grateful attachment as had been given to him in the northern and middle states.

The senate and congress had given to him the power of choosing a spot on which should be built a city for a seat of government, and he stopped at the Potomac for some days, and marked the place on which the city of Washington now stands. After his return from this journey, he said, in a letter to Mr. Gouverneur Morris—" In my late tour through the southern states, I experienced great satisfaction in seeing the good effects of the general government in that part of the Union. * * * Industry has there taken place of idleness, and economy of dissipation. Two or three years of good crops, and a ready market for the produce of their lands, have put every one in good humour; and, in some instances, they even impute to the government what is due only to the goodness of Providence.

In the December after his return, he heard the distressing intelligence of the total defeat of the army of General St. Clair, in an engagement with the Indians on the 4th of December, near the Miami river, in the state of Ohio.

When Washington heard of the destruction of the brave men and officers who fell in that battle, he went into a private room with one of his family, and indulged for a few moments his feelings of distress. He walked the floor with his hand pressed to his forehead, and said, "Here, in this very room, the night before his departure, I warned St. Clair to beware of surprise! and yet that brave army surprised and cut to pieces! Butler and a host of others slain!"

Washington's feelings were naturally violent when excited, but quickly subdued by the firmness with which he practised self-control. And after a few moments, he said, in a calm voice, "St. Clair shall have justice; yes, long, faithful, and meritorious services shall have their claims."

When the distressed St. Clair, worn down with age and disease, returned and visited him, he grasped the hand of Washington, which was kindly extended to him, and sobbed over it like a child. Many of the undeserved reproaches which were uttered against him, were silenced by the kind manner in which Washington continued to treat him.

After Congress adjourned, the president made another effort to form treaties of peace with the Indians, but was not successful; he then raised more troops, and the command of them was given to General Wayne, who soon succeeded in reducing the Indians to a state of submission and peace.

The rapidly increasing prosperity of the

United States, was a proof of the wisdom with which the new government had been planned, and was conducted. The good effect of Washington's wisdom and virtue were so apparent, that when the four years for which he had been elected were passed, the people proved that they knew the value of his character, and he was unanimously re-elected. He earnestly wished to return to private life, and expressed to his friends his intention to do so; but they convinced him that it was his duty not to indulge this wish; the state of public affairs at that time, requiring all his firm virtue to preserve the government from being engaged in the contentions which were commencing between the nations of Europe. When he met Congress after his re-election, his speech on the state of public affairs was deeply interesting, and contained this expression of pious feelings: " I humbly implore that Being on whose will the fate of nations depends, to crown with success our mutual endeavours for the general happiness."

The French revolution had commenced, and war was declared between England and France. Some Americans thought that their government ought to aid France against England, and the difference of opinion on this subject divided the people into two parties. But the president was not to be turned from his determination, to " cultivate peace with all the world;" and immediately after his re-election, he proclaimed that the American government would not take any part in the general war which had commenced. He thus secured for his country the rich blessing of peace ; and while war was raging amongst other nations, the Americans increased their trade, and sent large portions of their full harvests to different parts of the world.

The president was at times so much engaged that he could not allow himself time to take any other exercise than a walk to his watch maker's, in Second Street, to regulate his watch by the time-piece. Mothers who felt the value of what he had done for their children, watched for the hour in which it was usual for him to pass, and then brought out their children to show Washington to them. When the boys in the streets saw him, they used to cry out, " Here comes Washington ! here comes Washington !" they seldom called him the president. Washington was a far dearer name ; and he usually increased their delight by noticing them with a kind smile, giving them his hand, or taking the little children up in his arms. When he could be absent from the city for a few hours without neglecting a duty, he enjoyed a visit to Judge Peters, at his home on the Schuylkill, a few miles distant from Philadelphia. In the cultivated ground there, he planted a nut, which has grown into a thriving chestnut tree, and is cherished with great care. He was

fond of riding on horseback, and one day in
the winter, when the river Delaware was frozen, so that loaded sleds passed over it, he
crossed into Jersey to enjoy a ride in the
leafless woods. On his return, he found at
Cooper's ferry a farmer with a sled load of
wood, just going on the ice. The president
stopped his horse, to let the farmer pass on
before him. But the farmer, who knew
Washington, stopped also, and stepping up to
him, said respectfully—" Sir, do you think it
is right for you to run the risk of riding across
the river on the ice ?" " Why, my friend,"
said the president, " I think if you can pass over
with your sled load of wood without breaking
through, I have no reason to be afraid." "Ah,"
replied the farmer, " if I and a dozen like me,
should fall through and be drowned, we should
hardly be missed ; but the country *cannot do
without you, Sir.*" " Well, go on first then,"
said Washington, " and I think if the ice does
not break with your load and horses, I can
then pass it without danger." The farmer
moved on without delay, being, no doubt,
well pleased to serve Washington as a guide,
and to watch for the preservation of a life he
valued so highly.

In 1794, the second year after Washington's election, he had occasion to exercise his
firmness in quelling an insurrection excited
in the western parts of Pennsylvania by some
unprincipled idlers. Americans had resisted

with bravery and success, a foreign foe, but they had, and it is a sad truth, still have, an enemy in their homes, to which too many willingly submit, though by doing so they yield their right to the name of freemen ; for *strong drink* is a tyrant which chains the body in disgrace and poverty. It weakens the mind, and either destroys all recollection of the laws of God, or else causes a total disregard of them, and prepares the soul for everlasting punishment. Young Americans, this powerful foe is on every side of you, tempting you to become its slaves. Beware ! touch not, taste not *strong drink*, and when you see in others the evil effects of indulging in a love of it, let the bad example cause you sorrow, and prove a warning to you to begin in youth a firm resistance to such an enemy. It was this foe to good order and morality, that caused the insurrection which has been mentioned. Congress had laid a tax on spirits distilled within the United States, and some of the inhabitants of the western part of Pennsylvania, not only refused to pay the tax, but treated with violence those who were appointed to collect it. The disgraceful example was followed by so many, that it became necessary for the president to notice it. He endeavoured to make the rioters submit quietly to the laws, but when he found that they would not do so, he determined on sending against them a force which would be too pow-

erful for them to resist. By doing this he
hoped to prevent any blood being shed. Troops
were directed to assemble at Bedford, in
Pennsylvania ; and at Cumberland, on the
Potomac. Governor Lee, of Virginia, was
appointed to command the expedition, and as
the president had expected, the greatness of
the force subdued, without shedding blood,
the perverse spirit which had been raging.

During this season, the cares of Washington
were greater, perhaps, than at any other period
of his administration. The British government
had not given up their posts on the south side
of the lakes, which they had agreed to do in
the treaty of peace ; and the American government had violated the treaty, by passing some
laws, which had prevented English subjects
from recovering debts due to them in this
country,

Washington was just, and would not yield
to the clamour which was raised against the
English. He was of opinion, that " peace
ought to be pursued with unremitted zeal,"
while every necessary preparation should be
made for the preservation of national rights,
in case war could not be avoided. In writing
to a friend, after relating the various difficulties he had to contend with, he said,—" There
is but one straight course, and that is, to seek
the truth and pursue it steadily."

He appointed an ambassador to the English
government, for the purpose of endeavouring

to form a treaty. This ambassador was John Jay, who succeeded in forming a treaty, by which the English surrendered the posts on the south side of the lakes, and this enabled the president to protect the inhabitants of the frontiers from the Indians, and to promote the improvement and comfort of the Indians. for whom he was always interested. In recommending this subject to the attention of Congress, he said, that " As Americans were more powerful and enlightened than the Indians, they ought to treat them with kindness and liberality."

While Washington was pursuing that course of conduct towards the English government, which he knew would promote the interests of his country, he was severely tried by the party spirit which was growing strong in the minds of his countrymen, and which encouraged the French minister to behave in a very insolent manner towards the government. That minister, Mr. Genet, had arrived in Charleston in the year 1793, and he undertook to authorize the fitting out of armed vessels there, to capture the vessels of nations with whom the United States were at peace. An English merchant ship was also captured by a French privateer, within the capes of the Delaware, on her way from Philadelphia to the ocean.

The British minister complained of this, and also of the conduct of Genet; and the

council of the president unanimously agreed
that restitution should be made for the capture
of the English ship, and that Genet should
not be permitted to act again, as he had done
at Charleston. This displeased him greatly.
He had engaged two Americans to cruise from
that port; they were arrested, and he demand-
ed their release; not only of the magistrate,
but of the president, in a very insolent letter;
and, calculating on the support of the party in
favour of France, he insulted the government,
by appealing to the people against their president.

Washington directed Mr. Morris, the American minister, who was in France, to represent the conduct of Genet to his government,
and request that he should be recalled. The
request was complied with; but the party
feelings which had been excited, continued to
increase, and caused Washington's path to be
a thorny one. But, difficult as it was, he pursued steadily the great end which he had always in view, " the best interests of his country."

While he was deeply engaged in public business, he heard intelligence which pained his
heart. It was, that Lafayette had been driven
from his native land, by the unprincipled men
who were conducting the revolution there;
and that he had been seized in Prussia, and
sent to Austria; the emperor of which country directed that he should be confined in a

dungeon, in the town of Olmutz.   Washington could not interfere for his release, except
in the private character of his friend ; and he
used every means in his power to obtain it,
and wrote a letter to the emperor of Austria,
requesting him to permit Lafayette to come to
America, but his request was not granted.

A young German, named Bolman, and a
young American, named Huger, formed a
plan for effecting the escape of Lafayette. He
was sometimes permitted to leave his dungeon, and walk for a short distance with a
guard.   One day Bolman and Huger watched
for him, and had a horse ready, which Huger
led suddenly up to him, and desired him to
mount and escape ; the horse took fright and
ran off, Bolman followed to endeavour to catch
it, and Huger then insisted that Lafayette
should mount his horse ; he did so, and was
soon out of sight. Bolman could not overtake
the affrighted horse, and he returned and took
Huger behind him, and they followed Lafayette.

The guard gave the alarm, and they were
quickly pursued ; Huger was seized, but Bolman at that time escaped.   Lafayette was
stopped, and brought back to Olmutz.

Chained, hand and foot, Huger was carried
before a judge, who told him that it was probable his life would be the forfeit of his attempt to assist Lafayette to escape ; but that
possibly the emperor would treat him with

clemency, on account of his youth and motives. "Clemency!" said Huger, "how can
I expect it from a man who did not act even
with justice to Lafayette?" The judge said
to him, "If ever I need a friend, I hope that
friend may be an American." Huger suffered
from a close imprisonment for some time, and
was then allowed to return to his own country.

The efforts of Washington for the release
of his friend, did not cease, and perhaps the
letter which he wrote to the emperor had the
effect of lessening the severity with which
Lafayette had been treated, and of shortening
the period of his captivity. His son, named
George Washington, made his escape from
France, and arrived at Boston. The president
advised him to enter the University at Cambridge, and assured him that he would stand
in the place of a father to him, and become
his *friend*, *protector*, and *supporter*.

When the time came for a third election of
president, the people were again ready to
unite in voting for Washington. But he firmly
refused to be re-elected. He assured his countrymen that he did not do so from any want
of respect for their past kindness, or from
feeling less anxious for their future prosperity;—that he had twice yielded to their wishes,
because he thought that it was his duty to do
so, but felt that then the happy state of their
concerns would permit his retiring to enjoy

the quiet of his own home. As his determination was firm, they did not persist in opposing it, and he prepared to take again the character of a private citizen.

In concluding his last speech to Congress, (for Washington made his annual communications to Congress in a speech, instead of sending a written *message*, as his successors have done,) he said, " I cannot omit the occasion to repeat my fervent supplications to the Supreme Ruler of the universe and sovereign arbiter of nations, that his providential care may still be extended to the United States; that the virtue and happiness of the people may be preserved, and that the government, which they have instituted for the protection of their liberties, may be perpetual."

He also published a farewell address to the people of the United States, which contains the most instructive, important, and interesting advice, that was ever given by man to any nation. It is long, and has been often published, and splendidly engraved, and all young Americans should read it with attention, and make a firm determination that they will endeavour to follow the important and affectionate counsel, which the wise and virtuous Washington has left them as a legacy. He toiled through years of anxious cares to promote the happiness of his countrymen, and knowing that " sin is a disgrace to any people," but that " righteousness exalteth a nation," he earnestly entreated them to consider *religion* as the only lasting support of national prosperity.

When the Americans were convinced that Washington would retire from office, they elected John Adams, who was one of the signers of the Declaration of Independence, and who had served as vice-president during the whole term of Washington's presidency. Washington remained to offer his good wishes as a private citizen to the new president, and then immediately journeyed towards his home, which he was anxious to reach ; and, in a letter to a friend, he said, " To the wearied traveller, who sees a resting place, and is bending his body to lean thereon, I now compare myself."

Washington was ever ready to acknowledge the particular providence, and to adore the glorious character, of the Creator of heaven and of earth ; and therefore, when he rejoiced in the prosperity of his loved country, his heart could feel and offer the ascription. " Unto thee, O Lord, be all the glory and the praise."

CHAPTER XII

1796—1799.

THE rest for which Washington had longed, was not *idleness ;* and, when he had examined every part of his large farm, which had been in some degree neglected during his absence, he immediately commenced the employment of improving it.

His faithful mother, in forming his first habits, had not neglected that of early rising; and through the whole of his useful life that habit was continued; in winter, he rose usually two hours before day; and in summer, was ready to enjoy the healthful freshness and beauty of the dawn.

The habit of early rising, in connexion with the exemplary one of strict attention to order in all his employments, gave Washington "time for all things," so that even when he had numerous and arduous public duties to attend to, he did not neglect any private one, but performed with ease himself, what would seem to be employment for many. He was remarkably neat in his person, but used a very short portion of time for attention to his dress.

After his return to his farm, he visited his stables every day, to be certain that his horses were well taken care of. The one on which he rode when he was directing the siege of Yorktown, he did not use again; it was allowed to graze on the best pasture in summer, and was carefully stabled in winter, and died of old age, several years after the close of the war.

Washington was employed for several

hours, each day, in visiting all parts of his large farm. He went alone, opening and shutting the gates, and pulling down and putting up the bars as he passed.

One day, Colonel Meade, a valued friend of Washington, was met by Mr. Custis, a relation of Mrs. Washington; Colonel Meade inquired if he should find the General at the house, or if he was out on the farm. Mr. Custis, not knowing Colonel Meade, replied, that the General was out; and, giving directions as to the part of the farm on which he would probably be found, added, " You will meet, sir, with an *old gentleman, riding alone, in plain drab clothes, a broad brimmed white hat, a hickory switch in his hand, and carrying an umbrella, with a long staff, which is attached to his saddle-bow,—that, sir, is General Washington!*" The old friend of Washington replied, " Thank you, thank you, young gentleman; I think, if I fall in with the General, I shall be apt to know him."

This description of Washington gives us some knowledge of how he looked on his farm. So many pictures of him, in different situations, have been drawn,—and young Americans have so often seen him represented on sign-posts in every part of the land, that they think they know exactly how he looked; but unless they had seen him, instead of pictures of him, they can have no correct idea of his noble appearance.

In his youth he was remarkable for the straightness and manliness of his form, which was six feet and two inches high. The expression of his countenance was serious, but very pleasing; his eyes were a mild blue, and the flush of health gave a glow to his cheeks. His step was always firm; but after the toils of the long war, his body was a little bent as he walked, and his once smooth forehead and cheeks were wrinkled.

The venerable Charles Wilson Peale, who was the founder of the Philadelphia Museum, and lived to enter his eighty-sixth year, drew a likeness of him, when he was Colonel Washington, in the service of the king of England; and another, when he was the president of the free United States.

The river Potomac which flows by Mount Vernon, mingles with the Shenandoah river, at Harper's Ferry, and presents a scene wild and grand. There, the Shenandoah, after ranging from the south a hundred miles along the foot of the Blue Ridge, flows into the Potomac, and the united streams roll calmly on towards the ocean, with the name of Potomac, and give variety to the landscape of a level country, which is seen like a distant picture, through the opening in the Blue Ridge.

At a great height, the surface of the wall of rock is broken in the form of a human head, and the profile can be plainly traced. Travellers, who stop to gaze at the grand scenery around, are told that this profile on the rock resembles that of Washington ; and Americans who look at it, can readily and fondly think, that they see a likeness of him, where the hand of man can never reach to deface it.

At Harper's Ferry are extensive public works, for making military arms. If his countrymen regard and follow the important farewell counsel of Washington, to " *Observe good faith and justice towards all nations, and to cultivate peace and harmony with all*," these arms will not be used, except as weapons of defence ; and then not until "the cup of reconciliation is exhausted to the last drop."

A weekly school is kept at Harper's Ferry, for the children of the workmen, and they have the blessing of Sunday-school instruction.

Had Washington lived to the time when there are Sunday-schools in almost every portion of his native land, no doubt he would have rejoiced to see the children taught to know their Creator as he has revealed himself in his word,—to fear, obey, and love him, —and thus secure the blessing of " the faithful God, who keepeth covenant and mercy with them that love him and keep his commandments, to a thousand generations."

Washington said, " Of all the dispositions and habits which lead to political prosperity, religion and morality are indispensable supports."   Certainly, then, he. would have ap-

proved of children being taught the pure precepts of the gospel, and trained to restrain
those natural dispositions, which, if indulged,
would make them in manhood, useless or
vicious members of the community. He also
said, that " without an humble imitation of the
example of the divine Author of our blessed
religion, we cannot hope to be a happy nation." And as Washington always acted as
if he believed what he expressed, he would
have encouraged the effort to place in every
family of his country the Bible, which teaches
what that Divine example was, and how to
obtain that " new heart," and " right spirit,"
which delights in following it. The active
interest in behalf of Sunday-schools, displayed
by that revered man, who bore the name
and succeeded to the estate of Washington,
favours such a presumption. He who followed so closely the habits of his honoured
relative, and who maintained his principles,
so rigidly, was, to the day of his death, an
ardent friend to this system of universal edu-
cation. He considered, to use his own language, a society constituted for the promotion
of this great object, as entitled to be " called
the Charitable Society, as it diffused most per-
manently, the greatest amount of good."

The wants of the poor were not neglected
by Washington. He contributed liberally to
the support of schools for the children of the

indigent; and the sick and aged could bear
testimony to the benevolence of his heart.

On his farm he had a comfortable house
built for an old English soldier, who had
been an attendant of General Braddock, at
the time of his defeat; after his death, he entered into the service of Washington, and continued in it until the close of the provincial
war; he then married, and a home was provided for him at Mount Vernon. He was too
old to follow his beloved commander in the
struggle for independence, and was left at
home to enjoy the comforts which old age requires.   Children loved to visit the old soldier, and listen to his tales of the Indian war,
which he delighted in telling. When Washington was passing round his farm, he often stopped to gladden the heart of the gray-headed ve-
teran with kind words; and he lived to enjoy
the comforts which had been provided for him
until he was eighty years of age.

The days of Washington were spent in useful employments, and his evenings in the enjoyment of domestic happiness.   It was
then his custom to read to his family such
new publications as interested him, and on Sunday evenings the Bible and a sermon.   Sometimes he would sit, as if he forgot that he was
not alone, and raising his hand, would move
his lips silently, as if engaged in prayer.   In
town or country, he was a constant attendant
upon public worship, and by his devout de-

portment there, proved that he went there for the purpose of worshipping God. He always acknowledged by his example, that he felt his solemn obligation to keep holy the Sabbath day ; and to influence others to do so as far as was within his power.

His nephew, Bushrod Washington, was elected in the year 1826, a vice-president of the American Sunday School Union. He resided at Mount Vernon, which was left to him by his illustrious uncle. In a part of his answer to the letter which informed him of his election, he wrote thus : " I beg leave now to express the grateful sense I have of the honour conferred upon me, by the American Sunday School Union, in electing me one of the vice-presidents of that institution, and of the approbation bestowed by the Board of Managers upon the well intended efforts which I have made to secure the due observance of the sabbath day, upon a spot, where I am persuaded, it was never violated, during the life, and with the permission of its former venerable and truly Christian owner."

General Washington said, that " both reason and experience forbid us to expect that morality can prevail to the exclusion of religious principle;" and this sentiment is well supported by Chief-Justice Hale of England, who said, " that of all the persons who were convicted of capital crimes, while he

was upon the bench, he found a few only,
who would not confess, on inquiry, that they
began their career of wickedness by *a neglect
of the duties of the Sabbath, and a vicious
conduct on that day.*" And no doubt, the
prisons of our own country could produce a
host of witnesses to testify the same.   Then
the example of Washington in remembering
" the sabbath day, to keep it holy," was that
of a patriot as well as a Christian.

The peaceful life of Washington on his
farm was again disturbed by a call from his
countrymen to become their leader in the defence of their national rights.   The French
republic had refused to receive General Pinckney, a highly respected American, whom
Washington had sent to France as minister in
the year 1796.   He was ordered to quit the
territories of France, and at the same time
that the French republic expressed great attachment to the people of the United States
they abused the government, and thus showed
an intention to endeavour to separate the people from their government.   They also captured American vessels wherever they were
found.   The government of the United States
appointed three envoys, one of whom was
General Pinckney, to endeavour to preserve
peace " on terms compatible with the rights,
duties, interests, and honour of the nation."

In the spring of 1798, they informed their
government that they had entirely failed, and

were treated in a very insulting manner. Two of them were ordered to quit France, one was permitted to remain.

Congress determined on raising an army, and though they regretted to deprive the venerable Washington of that rest which he had earned by his past services, they complied with the wishes of his countrymen, and requested him to accept the command of the army. He did so, but continued to employ himself on his farm, being ready at any moment to obey a call to the duties of his appointment. But his Creator was soon about to call him from all earthly duties. We have now to proceed to the melancholy task of giving an account of the last sickness and the death of the Father of his Country. And this cannot be done better than in the words of Tobias Lear, one of his attendants, who drew up the following statement, on the day after the General's death. We have no fear that any of our readers will think the details too particular:

" On Thursday, December 12, the General rode out to his farm at about ten o'clock, and did not return home till past three. Soon after he went out, the weather became very bad; rain, hail, and snow falling alternately, with a cold wind. When he came in, I carried some letters to him to frank, intending to send them to the post-office. He franked the letters, but said the weather was too bad to send a servant to the office that evening. I observed to him that I was afraid he had got wet; he said no—his great coat had kept him dry; but his neck appeared to be wet—the snow was hanging to his hair.

" He came to dinner without changing his dress. In the evening he appeared as well as usual. A heavy fall of snow took place on Friday, which prevented the General from riding out as usual. He had taken cold, (undoubtedly from being so much exposed the day before,) and complained of having a sore throat; he had a hoarseness, which increased in the evening, but he made light of it, as he would never take any thing to carry off a cold,—always observing, " let it go as it came." In the evening, the papers having come from the post office, he sat in the room, with Mrs. Washington and myself, reading them, till about nine o'clock ; and, when he met with any thing which he thought diverting or interesting, he would read it aloud. He desired me to read to him the debates of the Virginia Assembly, on the election of a senator and governor, which I did. On his retiring to bed, he appeared to be in perfect health, except the cold, which he considered as trifling—he had been remarkably cheerful all the evening.

" About two or three o'clock on Saturday morning, he awoke Mrs. Washington, and informed her he was very unwell, and had an ague. She observed that he could scarcely speak, and breathed with difficulty, and she wished to get up and call a servant; but the General would not permit her, lest she should take cold. As soon as the day appeared, the woman Caroline went into the room to make a fire, and the girl desired that Mr. Rawlins, one of the overseers, who was used to bleeding the people, might be sent for to bleed him before the Doctor could arrive. I was sent for—went to the General's chamber, where Mrs. Washington was up, and related to me his being taken ill between two and three o'clock, as before stated. I found him breathing with difficulty, and hardly able to utter a word intelligibly. I went out instantly, and wrote a line to Dr. Plask, and sent it with all speed. Immediately I returned to the General's chamber, where I found him in the same situation I had left him. A mixture of molasses, vinegar, and butter, was prepared, but he could not swallow a drop; whenever he attempted it he was distressed, convulsed, and almost suffocated.

" Mr. Rawlins came in soon after sunrise, and prepared to bleed him; when the arm was ready the General observing Rawlins appeared agitated, said, with difficulty, " don't be afraid;" and, after the incision was made, he observed the orifice was not large enough—however the blood ran pretty freely. Mrs. Washington, not knowing whether bleeding was proper in the General's situation, begged that much blood might not be taken from him, and desired me to stop it. When I was about to untie the string, the General put up his hand to prevent it, and, so soon as he could speak, said " more."

" Mrs. Washington being still uneasy lest too much blood should be taken, it was stopped, after about half a pint had been taken. Finding that no relief could be obtained from bleeding, and that nothing could be swallowed, I proposed bathing the throat externally with sal volatile, which was done ; a piece of flannel was then put around his neck. His feet were also soaked in warm water, but it gave no relief. By Mrs. Washington's request, I despatched a messenger for Dr. Brown, at Port Tobacco. About 9 o'clock Dr. Craik arrived, and put a blister of flies on the throat of the General, and took more blood, and had some vinegar and hot water set in a teapot for him to draw in the steam from the spout.

" He also had sage tea and vinegar mixed and used as a gargle, but, when he held back his head to let it run down, it almost produced suffocation. When the mixture came out of his mouth some phlegm followed it, and he would attempt to cough, which the Doctor encouraged, but without effect. About eleven o'clock Dr. Dick was sent for. Dr. Craik bled the General again, but no effect was produced, and he continued in the same state, unable to swallow any thing. Dr. Dick came in about three o'clock, and Dr. Brown arrived soon after; when, after consultation, the General was bled again, the blood ran slowly, appeared very thick, and did not produce any symptoms of fainting. At four o'clock the General could swallow a little. Calomel and tartar emetic were administered without effect. About half past four o'clock he desired me to ask Mrs. Washington to come to his bedside, when he desired her to go down to his room and take from his desk two wills which she would find there, and bring them to him, which she did; upon looking at one, which he observed was useless, he desired her to burn it, which she did, and then took the other and put it way; after this was done I returned again to his bed side and took his hand: He said to me, "I find I am going— my breath cannot continue long: I believed from the first attack it would be fatal. Do you arrange and record all my military letters and papers; arrange my accounts and settle my books, as you know more about them than any one else; and let Mr. Rawlins finish recording my other letters, which he has begun." He asked when Mr. Lewis and Washington would return? I told him I believed about the 20th of the month. He made no reply to it.

"The physicians came in between five and six o'clock, and, when they came to his bedside, Dr. Craik asked him if he would sit up

in the bed: he held out his hand to me and
was raised up, when he said to the physician
—" I feel myself going; you had better not
take any more trouble about me, but let me go
off quietly; I cannot last long." They found
what had been done was without effect; he
laid down again, and they retired, excepting
Dr. Craik. He then said to him—" Doctor,
I die hard, but I am not afraid to go; I believed, from my first attack, I should not sur-
vive it; my breath cannot last long." The
doctor pressed his hand, but could not utter a
word; he retired from the bedside and sat by
the fire, absorbed in grief. About eight o'clock
the physicians again came into the room, and
applied blisters to his legs, but went out without a ray of hope. From this time he appeared
to breathe with less difficulty than he had
done, but was very restless, continually changing his position, to endeavour to get ease. I
aided him all in my power, and was gratified
in believing he felt it, for he would look upon
me with eyes speaking gratitude, but unable
to utter a word without great distress. About
ten o'clock he made several attempts to speak
to me before he could effect it; at length he
said, " I am just going. Have me decently
buried; and do not let my body be put into
the vault in less than two days after I am
dead." I bowed assent. He looked at me
again, and said, " Do you understand me?"
I replied, " Yes, sir." " 'Tis well," said he.

About ten minutes before he expired, his breathing became much easier—he lay quietly—he withdrew his hand from mine and felt his own pulse. I spoke to Dr. Craik, who sat by the fire; he came to the bedside. The General's hand fell from his wrist; I took it in mine and placed it on my breast. Dr. Craik placed his hands over his eyes, and he expired without a struggle or a sigh." His loved wife kneeled beside his bed, with her head resting on the Bible, in which she daily read the precepts, and cheering promises of her Saviour; and they comforted her in her hour of deepest sorrow. Her miniature portrait was found on the bosom of Washington, where he had worn it for forty years.

The report of his death reached Congress before they knew of his sickness; and when they heard it, a solemn silence prevailed for several minutes; Judge Marshall, the present Chief Justice of the United States, observed, " This information is not certain, but there is too much reason to believe it true. After receiving intelligence of a national calamity so heavy and afflicting, the House of Representatives can be but ill-fitted for public business." He then moved an adjournment, and both houses adjourned until the next day. When Congress then met, Mr. Marshall proposed several resolutions; one of which was, " Resolved, That a committee, in conjunction with one from the Senate, be appointed, to consi-

der on the most suitable manner of paying honour to the memory of the man, first in war,
first in peace, and first in the hearts of his fellow-citizens."

The Senate addressed a letter to the president, in which they said, "Permit us, sir, to
mingle our tears with yours. On this occasion
it is manly to weep. To lose such a man, at
such a crisis, is no common calamity to the
world. Our country mourns a father. The
Almighty disposer of human events has taken
from us our greatest benefactor and ornament.
It becomes us to submit with reverence to
him 'who maketh darkness his pavilion.' "

The president returned an answer expressive of his sorrow for the death of Washing
ton, and in the conclusion of it, said, " His
example is now complete ; and it will teach
wisdom and virtue to magistrates, citizens and
men ; and not only in the present age, but in
future generations, as long as our history shall
be read."

The people throughout the United States
mourned for Washington. They had been
ever ready to unite in expressing their grateful attachment to him, and they felt that they
had indeed lost their greatest benefactor.

In his will, which was a just and benevolent one, he directed that his body should be
laid in a vault, at Mount Vernon ; and added,
" It is my express desire, that my corpse may

be intered in a private manner, without parade or funeral oration.''

The original family vault of General Washington was about three hundred yards south of the mansion, and consisted of a narrow excavation in the bank, arched over with brick and covered with sod. It was his design to have appropriated another spot to this purpose, and he actually selected one before his death. A few years since a brick tomb was built on the site thus selected. The front of the tomb is roughcast, and has a plain iron door inserted in a strong free-stone casement. Over the door is a stone panel, on which the following sentence is engraved:

"I AM THE RESURRECTION AND THE LIFE; HE THAT BELIEVETH IN ME, THOUGH HE WERE DEAD, YET SHALL HE LIVE."

The spot is enclosed with a brick wall, twelve feet high, and entered in front by an iron gateway, several feet in advance of the vault door. Over the gate is a plain slab inserted in the brick work, on which is inscribed the following sentence:

"WITHIN THIS ENCLOSURE REST THE REMAINS OF GENERAL GEORGE WASHINGTON."

CONCLUSION.*

WASHINGTON was born on the 22d February, in the year 1732, and died on the 14th December, 1799.

One hundred years have elapsed since he was a child in a country school. From the time he was thirteen years old, his manuscript school books have been preserved. He had then completed the study of arithmetic, and these books commence with geometry. All the writing is neat, and the geometrical figures drawn with accuracy. There is one book of an earlier date, containing thirty folio pages; many of which are filled with what he terms "Forms of Writing." They are notes of hand, bills of exchange, land warrants, deeds, wills, &c., carefully written; the most important words in large and varied characters, in imitation of a clerk's hand. Under the head of "*Rules of Behaviour in Company and Conversation*," one hundred and ten are written and numbered. A few will serve to show their general character, and may be useful to the young reader, as proofs of the early dili-

* The additional information contained in this conclu sion, has been selected from "The Life and Writings of Washington," in twelve volumes, by Jared Sparks, who had in his possession, for ten years, all the original public and private papers of Washington; and from these and other sources drew materials for his invaluable work, published in 1839.

gence of Washington in using every means in his power to polish his manners, cherish kind feelings, impress upon his memory his duties, and incite to continual self-discipline.

Selections from the Rules.

" In your apparel be modest, and endeavour to accommodate nature rather than to procure admiration ; keep to the fashion and habits of your equals, such as are civil and orderly with respect to times and places."

" Play not the peacock, looking everywhere about you to see if you be well decked, if your shoes fit well, if your stockings sit neatly, and clothes handsomely."

" Be not curious to know the affairs of others ; neither approach to those that speak in private."

" Come not near the books or writings of any one so as to read them, unless desired, nor give your opinion of them unasked ; also look not nigh when another is writing a letter."

" Read no letters, books, or papers in company ; but when there is a necessity for doing it, you must ask leave."

" Associate yourself with men of good quality if you esteem your own reputation ; for it is better to be alone than in bad company."

" Every action in company ought to be with some sign of respect to those present."

" Be not forward, but friendly and courteous; the first to salute, hear and answer; and be not pensive when it is a time to converse."

"Think before you speak, pronounce not imperfectly, nor bring out your words too hastily, but orderly and distinctly."

"Strive not with your superiors in argu·ment, but always submit your judgment to others with modesty."

"When another speaks, be attentive your-self, and disturb not the audience."

"Let your conversation be without malice or envy, for it is a sign of a tractable and com-mendable nature ; and in all causes of passion admit reason to govern."

"In dispute, be not so desirous to overcome as not to give liberty to each one to deliver his opinion ; and submit to the judgment of the major part, especially if they are judges of the dispute."

"Speak not injurious words, neither in jest nor earnest ; scoff at none, although they give occasion."

"Be not hasty to believe flying reports to the disparagement of any."

"Be not apt to relate news, if you know not the truth thereof. In discoursing of things you have heard, name not your author always. A secret, discover not."

"Speak not evil of the absent, for it is un·just."

"Detract not from others, neither be exces·sive in commending."

"Use no reproachful language against any one, neither curse nor revile."

"Mock not, nor jest at any thing of importance."

"When you deliver a matter, do it without passion, and with discretion, however mean the person be you do it to."

"Show not yourself glad at the misfortune of another, though he were your enemy."

"When a man does all he can, though it succeeds not well, blame not him that did it."

"Wherein you reprove another be unblamable yourself; for example is more prevalent than precept."

"Being to advise or reprehend any one, consider whether it ought to be in public, or in private; presently, or at some other time; in what terms to do it; and in reproving, show no signs of choler, but do it with sweetness and mildness."

"Take all admonitions thankfully, in what time or place soever given; but afterwards, not being culpable, take a time or place convenient to let him know it that gave them."

"Undertake not what you cannot perform, but be careful to keep your promise."

"Honour and obey your natural parents, although they be poor."

"When you speak of God, or his attributes, let it be seriously in reverence."

"Sublime matters treat seriously."

" Let your recreations be manful, not sin-ful."

" *Labour to keep alive in your breast that little spark of celestial fire called conscience.*'

Washington vigilantly obeyed this last counsel ; and endeavoured " to have always a conscience void of offence toward God and toward men." Self-discipline, thus early commenced and unweariedly persevered in, enabled him to control his naturally strong temper, and check his ardent feelings. And the mildness and propriety of his manners, the firm correctness with which he spoke and acted on all occasions, evinced that he was influenced through life by the code of rules formed in his boyhood ; and when a young fatherless nephew was under his care, in a letter of advice to him he said, " Your future character and reputation will depend very much, if not entirely, upon the habits and manners which you contract in the present period of your life. You should therefore be extremely cautious how you put yourself into the way of imbibing those customs which may tend to corrupt your manners, or vitiate your heart."

Excellent as was his code of maxims, the book which contains it shows that it was not the highest source from which the youthful writer sought aid to form a virtuous character ; for there also are transcribed selections of reli-

gious poetry; one of which written on Christmas day, commences thus:

> "Assist me, muse divine, to sing the morn,
> On which the Saviour of mankind was born."

The pious feelings which prompted the boy
of thirteen to employ his pen with this holy
theme, induced him in early manhood, when
under the English government he commanded
a portion of the army, to apply earnestly for
chaplains to perform divine service regularly;
and in his orders to desire the officers "to
punish severely any man whom they should
hear swear, or make use of an oath." And
when he was at the head of the American
army, influenced by the same feelings, in
giving orders to the commanding officers of
each regiment to procure chaplains, he directed
that they should see that all inferior officers
and soldiers should pay them suitable respect;
and added, "The blessing and protection of
Heaven are at all times necessary; but especially so in times of public distress and danger.
The general hopes and trusts that every officer
and man will live and act as becomes a Christian soldier, defending the dearest rights and
liberties of his country." After expressing
sorrow that the "foolish and wicked practice
of profane cursing and swearing had become
common; and a hope that the officers would
by their example as well as influence, check it,
be said, "And that both they and the men

will reflect—that we can have little hope of
the blessing of Heaven on our arms, if we insult it by our impiety and folly. Added to this,
it is a vice so mean and low, without any
temptation, that every man of sense and character detests and despises it."

In his sixteenth year, the last summer that
he was at school, he surveyed the fields around
the school-house; and those of the adjoining
plantations, entered the result carefully in a
book, used logarithms, and proved the accuracy of his work by different methods.   He
thus filled several quires of paper, in which
there are no blots; the diagrams are beautiful,
and the tables and columns of figures arranged
with precision.   Through his busy life he felt
the benefit of his early methodical habits.   All
his business-papers and letter-books are without blemishes; and are excellent specimens
of exactness.   His original papers, including
his own letters and those which he received,
amount to more than two hundred folio volumes.   They now belong to the American
nation; for they have been purchased by Congress, and deposited in the archives of the de-
partment of state at the seat of government.
His earliest compositions were incorrect in
their grammatical construction, and prove that
he was not taught at school the principles of
language; but he perseveringly tried to improve himself by study, reading and practice,
until he wrote correctly, and used the most

appropriate words to express his thoughts And it has been remarked that " His language may be said to have reflected the image of his mind, in which candour, sincerity, and direct-ness were prevailing traits." His assiduity was no doubt very gratifying to his anxious mother, who could not procure for him the aid of a learned instructor; but she religiously inculcated in his childhood those virtuous principles without which the most learned edu-cation is useless. Her son proved, by his love and respect, his gratitude for her pious solici-tude. When she died, he was President of the United States; he was recovering from a se-vere illness, and wrote thus to his sister: " Aw-ful and affecting as the death of a parent is, there is consolation in knowing that Heaven has spared us ours to an age beyond which few attain, and favoured her with the enjoy-ment of her mental faculties, and as much bodily strength as usually falls to the lot of fourscore. Under these considerations, and a hope that she is translated to a happier place, it is the duty of her relatives to yield submis-sion to the decrees of the Creator."

Knowing and feeling the importance of edu-cation, he was always anxious to promote it, and when, soon after the war, he was chosen Chancellor of William and Mary College in Virginia, in his answer to the trustees accept-ing the appointment, he said, " I rely fully on your strenuous endeavours for placing the sys-

tem on such a basis as will render it most
beneficial to the state and the republic of letters,
as well as to the more extensive interests of
humanity and *religion*." In several instances
he offered to pay the expenses of young men
through a collegiate course. And for many
years gave annually fifty pounds for the instruction of poor children in Alexandria; and
in his will left a legacy of four thousand dollars, the income of which was to be thus applied forever. He always remembered the
poor. When Mrs. Washington was with him
in the camp, he wrote to the person who had
the care of his farm: "Let the hospitalities
of the house with respect to the poor be kept
up. Let no one go hungry away." He then
directed that those who wanted corn should be
supplied, provided it should not encourage
them in idleness; and that forty or fifty pounds
should be expended for the relief of the needy.
It has been said of him, that "the character
of his mind was unfolded in the public and
private acts of his life; and the proofs of his
greatness are seen almost as much in one as
the other." When he was at the head of the
army, and at the height of his power, a proposal was made to him to take the title of king;
in his answer to the officer through whom it
was made, he said, "Be assured, sir, no occurrence in the course of the war has given me
more painful sensations than your information
of there being such ideas existing in the army

as you have expressed, and I must view with abhorrence, and reprehend with severity." He always formed his determinations deliberately, and then used his power with firmness, when he knew that by doing so he should be acting as " the Father of his country" in promoting its prosperity : and when addresses were sent to induce him to refuse to sign the treaty which he had appointed Mr. Jay to negotiate with England ; in his answer to one he said, " While I feel the most lively gratitude for the many instances of approbation from my country, I can no otherwise deserve it than by obeying the dictates of my conscience." And in a letter to a friend he said, " The good citizen will look beyond the applauses and reproaches of men, and, persevering in duty, stand firm in conscious rectitude, in the hope of approving Heaven."* There is a natural fearlessness of danger, which is miscalled courage, when it induces a selfish disregard of the welfare of others. Courage, physical and moral, was a part of the nature of Washington; but his highest *ambition* was to promote the happiness of mankind ; and the noble sentiments of this humane hero were thus expressed in a letter to a French nobleman. " Your young military men who want to reap a harvest of laurels, do not care, I suppose, how many seeds of war are sown ; but, for the sake of humanity, it is devoutly to be wished that the

* See page 236.

manly employment of agriculture, and the humanizing benefits of commerce would supersede the waste of war, and the rage of conquest; that the swords might be turned into ploughshares, and the spears into pruning hooks; and, as the Scriptures express it, 'the nations learn war no more.'" On another occasion he said, "My first wish is to see the whole world in peace, and the inhabitants of it as a band of brothers, striving who should contribute most to the happiness of mankind."* He knew that this could be effected only by the universal influence of the precepts of Jesus, the Divine "Prince of Peace;" and in answering the address of the clergy and laity of the Episcopal church, presented when he was first elected president, he said, "On this occasion it would ill become me to conceal the joy I have felt in perceiving the fraternal affection which appears to increase every day among the friends of genuine religion. It affords edifying prospects indeed, to see Christians of every denomination dwell together in more charity, and conduct themselves in respect to each other with a more Christian spirit than

* Mr. Erskine, afterwards Lord Erskine, addressed to Washington a letter, dated London, March 15, 1795, in which he said, "I have a large acquaintance among the most valuable and exalted classes of men; but you are the only human being for whom I ever felt an awful reverence. I sincerely pray God to grant a long and serene evening to a life so gloriously devoted to the universal happiness of the world."

ever they have done in any former age, or in any other nation."

The various addresses he received then, and his answers, fill three manuscript volumes. The close of his answer to the ministers of one religious denomination, will show the feelings which influenced him in replying to all; he said, "I assure you I take in the kindest part the promise you make of presenting your prayers at the throne of grace for me; and that I likewise will implore the divine benediction on yourselves and your religious community." This declaration of Washington was not an unmeaning profession, and no doubt he literally fulfilled this promise to pray for those whose prayers for him were proffered. He was in the habit of communing with God, or he would not have made such an engagement. His practice was always in conformity with the opinions and feelings he expressed, and he had evinced his sentiments on Christian unity of spirit when the American army lay encamped at Morristown. He called on the Rev. Dr. Jones, the pastor of the Presbyterian church of that village, and said, "Dr., I understand that the Lord's supper is to be celebrated with you next Sunday; I would learn if it accords with the canon of your church to admit communicants of another denomination?" The doctor replied, "Most certainly; ours is not the Presbyterian table, general, but the Lord's table; and we hence give the Lord's invitation to all his followers, of whatever name." The general replied, " I am glad of it, that is as it ought to be; but as I was not quite sure of the fact, I thought I would ascertain it from yourself as I propose to join with you on that occasion Though a member of the Church of England, I have no exclusive partialities." Dr. Jones assured him of a cordial welcome, and he took his seat with the communicants on the next Sabbath. Early in life, he was actively interested in church affairs; was a vestryman of Truro parish, in which was Pohick church, seven miles from Mount Vernon. He was also a vestryman in Fairfax parish, the place of worship of which was in Alexandria, ten miles from his home. He had a pew in each church. On a day appointed for fasting, humiliation and prayer, he wrote in his diary, " Went to church and *fasted all day.*" Conforming not only to the spirit, but strictly to the letter of the appointment. His private devotional habits were in accordance with his invariable public ones. He usually rose at four o'clock and went into his library. His nephew, Mr. Robert Lewis, who was his private secretary when he was president, said that he had accidentally witnessed his private devotions both morning and evening; that on those occasions he had seen him in a kneeling posture, with a Bible open before him; and that he believed such to have been his daily practice. He adopted a grand-daughter of Mrs. Washington, and she resided in his family twenty years. In a letter, dated 1833, that lady wrote of Washington thus: "It was his custom to retire to his library at nine or ten o'clock, where he remained an hour before he went to his chamber. He always rose before the sun, and remained in his library until called to breakfast. I never witnessed his private devotions. I never inquired about them. I should have thought it the greatest heresy to doubt his firm belief in Christianity. His life, his writings, prove that he was a Christian. He was not one of those who act or pray 'that they may be seen of men;' he communed with his God in secret. * * * When my aunt, Miss Custis, died suddenly at Mount Vernon, before they could realize the event, he knelt by her and prayed most fervently, most affectionately, for her recovery. He was a silent, thoughtful man. He spoke little, generally never of himself. I never heard him relate a single act of his life during the war." After some other remarks, she mentions her grandmother thus: " He knew that I had the most perfect model of female excellence ever with me, as my monitress, who acted the part of a tender and devoted parent, loving me only as a mother can love, and never extenuating, or approving in me what she disapproved in others. She never omitted her private devotions or her public duties; and she and her husband were so perfectly united and happy that he must have been a Christian.* She had no doubts, no fears for him. After forty years of devoted affection and uninterrupted happiness, she resigned him without a murmur into the arms of his Saviour and his God, with the assured hope of his eternal felicity. Is it necessary that any one should certify General Washington avowed himself to me a believer in Christianity? as well may we question his patriotism, his heroic disinterested devotion to his

* In the first year of Washington's presidency, Mrs. Washington wrote to a friend thus : " I little thought when the war was finished that any circumstances could possibly happen that would call the general into public life again. I had anticipated that from that moment we should be suffered to grow old together in solitude and tranquillity. That was the first and dearest wish of my heart. I will not, however, contemplate with too much regret, disappointments that were inevitable, though his feelings and my own were in perfect unison with respect to our predilection for private life. Yet, I cannot blame him for having acted according to his ideas of duty in obeying the voice of his country. * * * * With respect to myself, I sometimes think the arrangement is not quite as it ought to have been, that I who had much rather be at home, should occupy a place with which a great many younger and gayer women would be extremely pleased. * * * * * I do not say this because I feel dissatisfied with my present station, for everybody and every thing conspire to make me as contented as possible in it ; yet, I have learned too much of the vanity of human affairs, to expect felicity from the scenes of public life. I am still determined to be cheerful and happy in whatever situation I may be ; for I have also learned from experience, that the greater part of our happiness or misery depends on our dispositions, and not on our circumstances. We carry the seeds of the one or the other about with us in our minds wherever we go."

country. His mottoes were, 'DEEDS, NOT WORDS; and, FOR GOD AND MY COUNTRY.'"

This truly great man, when he was dying, evinced tender solicitude for the comfort of others. His African servant, Christopher, had been for some time standing in his room, and was directed by him to sit down. Mr. Lear, who was on the bed endeavouring to assist him, when he wished to change his posture, said, "He appeared penetrated with gratitude for my attentions, and often said, 'I am afraid I shall fatigue you too much;' and upon my assuring him that I could feel nothing but a wish to give him ease, he replied, 'Well, it is a debt we must pay to each other, and I hope when you want aid of this kind you will find it.' His patience, fortitude, and resignation, never forsook him for a moment. In all his distress he uttered not a sigh nor a complaint; always endeavouring, from a sense of duty as it appeared, to take what was offered to him, and to do as he was desired by the physicians."

Young reader, you have learned why there was cause for joy in WASHINGTON's birth-day, and for sorrow in the day of his death. If you have been attentive to what you have read of his conduct, from the one day to the other, you know that in childhood he was a lover of truth, and a peacemaker among his schoolmates;— that in boyhood he was a diligent scholar, and the leader of his companions—not in mischief, folly, or vice —but in harmless and healthy exercises: and was a pattern of obedience to the wishes of a parent:—that, when the years of boyhood were passed, he immediately applied to useful purposes the knowledge which he had acquired by attention to instruction; and that early in manhood, he merited the confidence of the government of his native Province, and was intrusted with important and dangerous duties, which he performed with faithful perseverance;—that he used all his talents, and spent almost all his years, from manhood to declining age, in the service and for the benefit of his fellow-beings; and even in old age, was willing to yield the peaceful enjoyments which he loved most, because he thought that it was "the duty of every person, of every description, to contribute, at all times, to his country's welfare."

Through all his course of trials and temptations, in adversity or prosperity, he was just industrious, temperate, honest, generous, brave, humane, modest,—a real lover of his country, and an humble worshipper of God. Was he not worthy of your imitation? Your station in life may be a lowly one, but if your home is even a log hut, you may be, like Washington, a lover of truth, temperate, industrious, just, humane, honest, submissive to the government of your country, and obedient to the commands of God, and grow up to be indeed *freemen,*—and to enjoy, under the protection of just laws, the comfortable subsistence which in this favoured land you may obtain for yourselves.

But, remember, Washington directed his countrymen to a higher example than his ; he said that he earnestly prayed they might follow that of " THE DIVINE AUTHOR OF OUR BLESSED RELIGION ;" and the Bible, the sacred book which makes known that example, you should value as the crown of all your blessings ; for in it, you may learn how to secure their continuance through this *short life*, and how to obtain that blissful gift of God, " *Eternal life*, through Jesus Christ, our Lord."

APPENDIX, (A.)

DECLARATION OF INDEPENDENCE.

In Congress, July, 4, 1776.

THE UNANIMOUS DECLARATION OF THE THIRTEEN
UNITED STATES OF AMERICA.

WHEN, in the course of human events, it becomes necessary for one people to dissolve the political bands which have connected them with another, and to assume, among the powers of the earth, the separate and equal station to which the laws of nature and of nature's God entitle them, a decent respect to the opinions of mankind requires that they should declare the causes which impel them to the separation.

We hold these truths to be self-evident:—that all men are created equal, that they are endowed by their Creator with certain unalienable rights; that among these are life, liberty, and the pursuit of happiness. That to secure these rights, governments are instituted among men, deriving their just powers from the consent of the governed; that whenever any form of government becomes destructive of these ends, it is the right of the people to alter or to abolish it, and to institute a new government, laying its foundation on such principles, and organizing its powers in such form as to them shall seem most likely to effect their safety and happiness. Prudence, indeed, will dictate, that governments long established should not be changed for light and transient causes; and accordingly all experience hath shown, that mankind are more disposed to suffer while evils are sufferable, than to right themselves by abolishing the forms to which they are accustomed. But when a long train of abuses and usurpations, pursuing invariably the same object, evinces a design to reduce them under absolute despotism, it is their right, it is their duty to throw off such government, and to provide new guards for their future security. Such has been the patient sufferance of these colonies; and such is now the necessity which constrains them to alter their former systems of government. The history of the present king of Great Britian is a history of repeated injuries and usurpations, all having in direct object the establishment of an absolute tyranny over these states. To prove this, let facts be submitted to a candid world.

He has refused his assent to laws the most wholesome and necessary for the public good.

He has forbidden his governors to pass laws of immediate and pressing importance, unless suspended in their operation, till his assent should be obtained; and when so suspended, he has utterly neglected to attend to them. He has refused to pass other laws for the accommodation of large districts of people, unless those people would relinquish the right of representation in the legislature—a right inestimable to them, and formidable to tyrants only.

He has called together legislative bodies at places unusual, uncomfortable, and distant from the repository of their public records, for the sole purpose of fatiguing them into compliance with his measures.

He has dissolved representative houses repeatedly, for opposing, with manly firmness, his invasions on the rights of the people.

He has refused, for a long time after such dissolutions, to cause others to be elected ; whereby the legislative powers, incapable of annihilation, have returned to the people at large, for their exercise, the state remaining, in the mean time, exposed to all the dangers of invasion from without, and convulsions within.

He has endeavoured to prevent the population of these states ; for that purpose obstructing the laws for naturalization of foreigners ; refusing to pass others to encourage their migration hither, and raising the conditions of new appropriations of lands.

He has obstructed the administration of justice, by refusing his assent to laws for establishing judiciary powers.

He has made judges dependent on his will alone

for the tenure of their offices, and the amount and payment of their salaries.

He has erected a multitude of new offices, and sent hither swarms of officers, to harass our people and eat out their substance.

He has kept among us, in times of peace, stand ing armies, without the consent of our legislatures.

He has affected to render the military independent of, and superior to, the civil power.

He has combined with others to subject us to a jurisdiction foreign to our constitution, and unacknowledged by our laws; giving his assent to their acts of pretended legislation :

For quartering large bodies of armed troops among us :

For protecting them, by a mock trial, from punishment for any murders which they should commit on the inhabitants of these states :

For cutting off our trade with all parts of the world :

For imposing taxes on us without our consent :

For depriving us in many cases, of the benefits of trial by jury :

For transporting us beyond seas to be tried for pretended offences :

For abolishing the free system of English laws in a neighbouring province, establishing therein an arbitrary government, and enlarging its boundaries, so as to render it at once an example and fit instrument for introducing the same absolute rule into these colonies :

For taking away our charters, abolishing our most valuable laws, and altering, fundamentally, the forms of our governments :

For suspending our own legislatures, and declaring themselves invested with power to legislate for us in all cases whatsoever.

He has abdicated government here, by declaring us out of his protection, and waging war against us.

He has plundered our seas, ravaged our coasts, burnt our towns, and destroyed the lives of our people.

He is at this time transporting large armies of foreign mercenaries to complete the works of death, desolation, and tyranny, already begun with circumstances of cruelty and perfidy, scarcely paralleled in the most barbarous ages, and totally unworthy the head of a civilized nation.

He has constrained our fellow-citizens, taken captive on the high seas, to bear arms against their country, to become the executioners of their friends and brethren, or to fall themselves by their hands.

He has excited domestic insurrections amongst us, and has endeavoured to bring on the inhabitants of our frontiers the merciless Indian savages, whose known rule of warfare is an undistinguished destruction of all ages, sexes, and conditions.

In every stage of these oppressions we have petitioned for redress in the most humble terms: our repeated petitions have been answered only by repeated injury. A prince, whose character is thus marked by every act which may define a tyrant, is unfit to be the ruler of a free people.

Nor have we been wanting in attentions to our British brethren. We have warned them, from time to time, of attempts by their legislature to extend an unwarrantable jurisdiction over us. We have reminded them of the circumstance of our emigration and settlement here. We have appealed to their native justice and magnanimity, and we have conjured them by the ties of our common kindred to disavow these usurpations, which would inevitably interrupt our connexions and correspondence. They too have been deaf to the voice of justice and of consanguinity. We must, therefore, acquiesce in the necessity which denounces our separation, and hold them, as we hold the rest of mankind—enemies in war, in peace friends.

We, therefore, the representatives of the United States of America, in general congress assembled, appealing to the Supreme Judge of the world, for the rectitude of our intentions, do, in the name and by the authority of the good people of these colonies, solemnly publish and declare, that these united colonies are, and of right ought to be, free and independent states ; that they are absolved from all allegiance to the British crown, and that all political connexion between them and the state of Great Britain is, and ought to be, totally dissolved; and that, as free and independent states, they have full power to levy war, conclude peace, contract alliances, establish commerce, and to do all other acts and things which independent states may of right do. And for the support of this declaration, with a firm reliance on the protection of Divine Providence, we mutually pledge to each other our lives, our fortunes, and our sacred honour.

JOHN HANCOCK.

NEW HAMPSHIRE.
Josiah Bartlett,
William Whipple,
Matthew Thornton.

MASSACHUSETTS BAY.
Samuel Adams,
John Adams,
Robert Treat Paine,
Elbridge Gerry.

RHODE ISLAND, &c.
Stephen Hopkins,
William Ellery.

CONNECTICUT.
Roger Sherman,
Samuel Huntington,
William Williams,

Oliver Wolcott.

NEW YORK.
William Floyd,
Philip Livingston,
Francis Lewis,
Lewis Morris.

NEW JERSEY.
Richard Stockton,
John Witherspoon,
Francis Hopkinson,
John Hart,
Abraham Clark.

PENNSYLVANIA.
Robert Morris,
Benjamin Rush,
Benjamin Franklin,

John Morton,
George Clymer,
James Smith,
George Taylor,
James Wilson,
George Ross.

DELAWARE.

Cæsar Rodney,
George Read,
Thomas M'Kean.

MARYLAND.

Samuel Chase,
William Paca,
Thomas Stone,
C Carroll, of Carrollton.

VIRGINIA.

George Wythe
Richard Henry Lee,

Thomas Jefferson
Benjamin Harrison,
Thomas Nelson, jr.
Francis Lightfoot Lee
Carter Braxton.

NORTH CAROLINA.

William Hooper,
Joseph Hewes,
John Penn.

SOUTH CAROLINA.

Edward Rutledge,
Thomas Heyward, jr.
Thomas Lynch, jr.
Arthur Middleton.

GEORGIA.

Button Gwinnett,
Lyman Hall,
George Walton.

APPENDIX. (B.)

The following is extracted from a letter addressed by the late Thomas McKean to C. A. Rodney

Philadelphia, Aug. 22d, 1813.

On Monday the 1st of July, 1776, the question
respecting independence was taken in the committee of the whole, when the State of Pennsylvania
(represented by seven gentlemen then present)
voted against it : Delaware (having then only two
representatives present) was divided: all the other
States voted in favour of it. Whereupon, without
delay, I sent an express for Cæsar Rodney, Esq.,
the remaining member for Delaware, whom I met
at the State-house door as the members were assembling. After a friendly salutation, (without a
word on the business,) we went into the Hall of
Congress together, and found we were among the
latest. Proceedings immediately commenced, and
after a few minutes the great question was put
When the vote for Delaware was called, your uncle
arose, and said : " As I believe the voice of my
constituents and of all sensible and honest men is
in favour of independence, and my own judgment
concurs with them, I vote for independence;" or

286

in other words to the same effect. The State of Pennsylvania on the 4th of July voted for it. Unanimity in the thirteen States, an all-important point on so great an occasion, was thus obtained; the dissension of a single State might have produced very dangerous consequences.

In the public journal of Congress for 1776, vol. II., it would appear that the Declaration of Independence was signed on the 4th of July by the members whose names are there inserted; but the fact is not so: for no person signed it on that day, nor for many days after. On the 4th of July, 1776, the Declaration of Independence was ordered to be engrossed on parchment, and then to be signed. I was not in Congress after the 4th, for some months having marched with my regiment of associators of this city, as colonel, to support General Washington until a flying camp of ten thousand men was completed. When the associators were discharged, I returned to Philadelphia, took my seat in Congress, and then signed the Declaration on parchment. Two days after, I went to Newcastle, and joined the Convention for forming a constitution for the future government of the State of Delaware, (having been elected a member for Newcastle county,) which I wrote in a tavern, without a book or any assistance.

You may rely on the accuracy of the foregoing relation. It is full time to print and publish the

APPENDIX, (C.)

REMINISCENCES OF GEN. WASHINGTON

And of the Congress, which sat in Philadelphia while he was President

AFTER a great deal of talking and writing, and controversy, about the permanent seat of Congress under the present Constitution, it was determined that Philadelphia should be honoured with its presence for ten years, and that afterwards its permanent location should be in the city of Washington, where it now is. In the mean time, the federal city was in progress, and the legislature of Pennsylvania voted a sum of money to build a house for the president, perhaps with some hopes that this might help to keep the seat of the general government in the capital—for Philadelphia was then considered the capital of the State. What is now the University of Pennsylvania was the structure used for this purpose. But as soon as General Washington saw its dimensions, and a good while before it was finished, he let it be known that he would not occupy it—that he should not certainly go to the expense of purchasing furniture for such a dwelling.

President Washington, therefore, rented a house
of Mr. Robert Morris, in Market street, between
Fifth and Sixth street, on the south side, and furnished it handsomely but not gorgeously.   There
he lived with Mrs. Washington; Mr. Lear his private secretary and his wife, and Mrs. Washington's
grandson, Custis, making a part of the family.
Young Custis had a private tutor employed by the
president, who was engaged to attend on his pupil
one hour in the winter mornings before breakfast;
and who then commonly breakfasted with the president and his family.

The company usually assembled in the drawing-
room, about fifteen or twenty minutes before dinner,
and the president spoke to every guest personally
on entering the room.   He always dressed in a
suit of black, his hair powdered, and tied in a black
bag behind, with a very elegant dress sword, which
he wore with inimitable grace.

Mrs. Washington often, but not always, dined
with the company, and if, as was occasionally the
case, there were other ladies present, they sat on
each side of her.   The president himself sat half
way from the head to the foot of the table, and on
that side which would place Mrs. Washington,
though distant from him, on the right hand.   He
always, unless a clergyman was present, asked a
blessing at his own table, in a standing posture.
If a clergyman was present, he was requested to

ask a blessing before, and return thanks after dinner.

The president, it is believed, generally dined on one dish, and that of a very simple kind. If offered something, either in the first or second course, which was very rich, his usual reply was, "That is too good for me."

Congress Hall was the building now occupied as a court-house, at the corner of Chestnut and Sixth street. Except a vestibule, about fifteen feet wide on Chestnut street, the whole of the ground floor of this building was formed into a hall or chamber for the House of Representatives.

There was no door opening into Sixth street, and the speaker's chair with two desks, the one on the right hand of the speaker for the clerk of the House, and the one on the left for the chaplain, were placed directly opposite to where the door of entrance from Sixth street is now placed. The chamber was warmed by large open stoves, commonly called Franklin stoves, two adjoining the wall on Sixth street, and two on the opposite wall. The fuel used was always of the best hickory wood. The house was entered by one door in Chestnut street —at the other end of the chamber there was a door eading into the State-house yard.

The Senate Chamber was directly over that of the House of Representatives: all stairways, commencing in the vestibule of the building, led to the

door of this chamber, which was but little more
than half as large as that of the other house—the
part (nearly one-half) towards Chestnut street,
being partitioned off, and divided into committee-
rooms, for the use of the members of both Houses,
and one room for their clerks.   The chair of the
vice-president was located on the south side of the
chamber, near the wall, and midway between the
eastern and western sides.   The arrangements
were the same as in the other chamber, except that
there were but two tiers of seats, both without ele-
vation, and in place of four stoves, the room had
but two.   The furniture, indeed, in this chamber,
was, in general, a little more showy than in the
other; but its great ornament consisted in the full-
length portraits of the King and Queen of France,
Louis XIV. and Marie Antoinette, under whose
reign our treaty of alliance with France, during our
revolutionary war, was formed.

These pictures were a royal present made to the
old Congress, and were of the most splendid kind.
It was said that the likenesses of the king and
queen were remarkably exact; but however this
might be, the paintings, as to the design, colouring,
and finishing, were the most perfect that had ever
been seen in the country—perhaps than any that
have since been seen, with the exception of the
crowning of Napoleon.   Both the king and the
queen appearing in their robes, or state-dress, and

nothing could exceed the exquisite tints and finish of the drapery. But the framing of the pictures was, in its kind, as singularly splendid as that which it enclosed. The frames of both, which were perhaps a foot and a half in width, were carved in a masterly manner, exhibiting the arms of France and other signs of royalty, and covered with a thick gilding, that had much the appearance of solid gold. The pictures hung on the opposite wall to that on which the vice-president's chair was placed, and fronting that chair. In the height of the French revolution there was some talk of removing or covering these pictures, but they remained till the transfer of Congress to Washington, and were never covered.

It was in the Senate Chamber, and in the presence of both Houses of Congress, that Washington delivered his speeches—for he did not send them by his secretary in the form of a message. This was a practice introduced by Mr. Jefferson, and has been continued ever since. But Washington made his communication at every opening of Congress in person. When informed that the houses were in session and ready to receive his communications, he replied to the committee that waited on him, that he would meet Congress the next day at twelve o'clock.

When he came into the Senate Chamber, the members all rose, and, bowing to them gracefully

294 REMINISCENCES OF WASHINGTON

he took his seat, and at the same time the members resumed theirs. He commonly sat about three or four minutes, during which time he took his spectacles from the side-pocket of his coat, and his speech from another pocket, and placed both on his knee, casting his eyes over the audience. He then put on his spectacles, took his speech in his left hand, rose, and immediately began to read, the members remaining seated. He read his speech audibly, distinctly, and without hesitation; he was not what could be called an accomplished reader. He occasionally, in an interesting part of his speech, enforced what he said by a motion with his right hand—the gesture was not violent, or even what is called bold; but it indicated earnestness, and was gracefully made. When he had finished his speech, he bowed to Congress, and the members rose while he retired.

APPENDIX, (D.)

THOSE who were personally familiar with these facts assure us, that not only the children, but the whole population were interested in his going out, and in his coming in. Shop-keepers left their counters, and mechanics their tools, and came where they might see him as he passed. And this was done, not with the rush and confusion common on like occasions, but it was altogether an expression of spontaneous respect and profound regard, and the word was passed indicating his approach.

THE END.

Reproduction also available from

ADAM'S CHART OF HISTORY
SEBASTIAN ADAMS

A vintage reproduction of this famous illustrated timeline of earth history first published in 1871. The fold-out chart features detailed, full-color drawings of various stages of history, from Adam and Eve to the late 19th century, with handwritten commentary throughout.

When opened, the accordian-style fold-out of the 21 full-sized panels make it a unique resource and an easy way to learn.

Discover ancient cultures like the Assyrians, Babylonians, Persians, Greeks, and more! Get the big picture history and how it falls in line with a biblical worldview!

$39.99
Case 21 panels
ISBN 13: 978-0-89051-505-1
RELIGION / Biblical Reference / General

Reproduction also available from

PILGRIM'S PROGRESS
JOHN BUNYAN

Includes:

The Pilgrim's Progress

Grace Abounding to the Chief of Sinners

Bunyan's Dying Sayings

The Holy War

The Barren Fig-Tree

Bunyan's Last Sermon

The Imprisonment and Release
of John Bunyan

Christian Behavior

The Water of Life

CHAPTER III.

ow, as Christian was walking solitary by himself, he espied one afar off, crossing over the field to meet him, and their hap was to meet just as they were crossing the way to each other. This gentleman's name was Mr. Worldly Wiseman: he dwelt in the town of Carnal Policy, a very great town, and also

$59.99
Casebound • 952 pages
ISBN 13: 978-0-89051-440-5
FICTION/Christian/Classic & Allegory

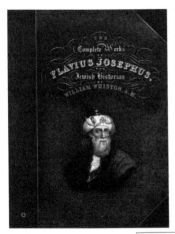

Reproduction also available from

LEONARD'S BIBLICAL CHRONOLOGICAL CHART
C. W. Leonard

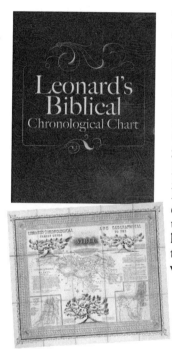

Filled with information in every edge, border, and ornate decoration, the chart includes several maps - the Middle East, Canaan according to the Syrian division, and the journeying of the Children of Israel from Egypt to Canaan. Other engravings include genealogical trees with the Kings of Judah, the Kings of Israel, and the family of Jacob. Religious historical events and explanations help enhance understanding of biblical history, and the voyages and travels of Paul are shared as well.

$14.99
Case 16 panels
Release Date: Feb 2010
ISBN 13: 978-0-89051-582-2
RELIGION/Biblical Reference/General